William Denny Brothers and the Hovercraft

Quentin Wilson

with acknowledgements to
Ted Tattersall

Published by the Scottish Maritime Museum
Scottish Charity Number SC 007133

First published 2013
The Scottish Maritime Museum
Laird Forge Buildings
Gottries Road
Irvine
Ayrshire KA12 8QE

www.scottishmaritimemuseum.org

British Library Cataloguing in Publication Data.
A catalogue record for this book is available from the British Library.

ISBN 978-0-9926652-0-3

Printed by
Minuteman Press Ayr
61 Kyle Street
Ayr KA7 1RS
U.K.

Contents

		Page
Foreword by Professor Dugald Cameron		*i*
Introduction		*ii*
Source Material and Acknowledgements		*v*
Chapter 1	Why "Hovercraft"?	1
Chapter 2	William Denny and Brothers - a record of Enterprise and Innovation	6
Chapter 3	The Basic Ideas behind the Original Hovercraft.	13
Chapter 4	The Denny D.1 and D.2 Hovercraft.	17
Chapter 5	Denny Hovercraft Limited.	28
Chapter 6	The Voyage of D.2-002 to London.	34
Chapter 7	The Thunderbolt and after.	41
Chapter 8	1964 onwards.	48
Chapter 9	The story of Hovermarine.	55
Chapter 10	A very brief Note on Flexible Skirts.	60
Chapter 11	Denny and Norwest Hovercraft.	64
Chapter 12	Other Hovercraft on the Clyde.	73
Chapter 13	What might have been!	78
References and Bibliography		87
Appendix 1	Early beginnings - the first Part of Ted's Newcomen Lecture.	88
Appendix 2	Notes on the 'Denny Hovercraft' film held by the Scottish Screen Archive.	94

Foreword

The Clydeside shipbuilding firm of William Denny and Brothers whose yard was sited at the confluence of the Rivers Leven and Clyde at Dumbarton took an enlightened view of research, and was notable for its record of innovation and acceptance of new ideas. It is not, therefore, surprising that it got interested in hovercraft, sadly too near the firm's closure in 1963, a decade which saw the beginnings of the demise of many of the yards which had previously built so much of the world's shipping. Denny had specialised in coastal steamers and ferries. In Sir Maurice Denny, in the later years of the company, they had someone who amongst other educational achievements had studied at the Massachusetts Institute of Technology, the famous M.I.T.

Denny's had an experimental test tank where they could evaluate hull hydrodynamics and investigate ship propeller design. Moving from ship's propellers to aircraft was a fairly natural progression and this they did quite spectacularly in the form of an experimental helicopter which appeared in 1905. This was the brainchild of Edwin R. Mumford with J. Pollock Brown and it eventually 'flew' tethered from 1909. WW1 saw the end of the adventure, though a second machine had been constructed - a similar fate to that which befell the successful Weir helicopters of 1938/9 - what if only?

This is a rather long way of saying that getting interested in hovercraft might be regarded as quite natural to Denny's, though another fifty or so years later on!

The hovercraft like many clever inventions and innovations was perhaps greeted over enthusiastically, initially. It was, and is indeed, a very good answer to some specialised transport needs, though its reception by the Royal Navy and the Royal Air Force seemed to echo that of the aeroplane prior to WW1 - the Navy regarded it as an aircraft and nothing to do with them and the Air Force as a ship and, therefore, nothing to do with them, so it took some exercise in that peculiarly British sort of bureaucracy to come to a kind of agreement as to what it actually was, officially, or is that a nice myth?

This account of the Denny Hovercraft development by Quentin Wilson, incorporating the late Ted Tattersall's work, could not have been produced by anyone better placed to give it for both were in there at first hand, in Ted Tattersall's case as an associate of Sir Christopher Cockerell, the inventor of the modern Hovercraft, and Quentin Wilson's as being intimately involved with the Denny craft.

The book reflects Quentin's meticulous approach to any task and is a welcome and much needed addition to the story of Clydeside engineering. A nice touch is the inclusion of Quentin's sketch of the Clyde turbine steamer *Queen Mary II* passing John Brown's yard while on its way down river.

Quentin Wilson is an Ayrshire lad from Maybole, educated there and at the University of Glasgow and the College of Aeronautics, Cranfield. He joined Vickers Armstrongs (Aircraft), then William Denny and Brothers at Dumbarton - his experiences there working on hovercraft developments are part of the subject of this book. After the sad demise of Denny's, he joined the Hovercraft Division of Vickers, following that in 1966 by lecturing at Robert Gordon's Institute of Technology in Aberdeen. Finally he joined British Aerospace / BAE Systems at Prestwick as a stress engineer on the Jetstream 41 project, when he dealt with aspects of the strength of the aircraft's wing and other certification matters, finally seeing the project progress from launch to maturity. He was one of the small team at Prestwick which built the Pilcher replica glider now on display in the Riverside Museum in Glasgow. He retired in 2002 at 67 years of age. At the time of writing he is the energetic Lecture Secretary of the Prestwick Branch of the Royal Aeronautical Society.

Professor Dugald Cameron OBE DSc

Introduction

On Tuesday 23rd July 1963 it was announced that the long-established and highly-regarded shipbuilding company of William Denny and Brothers had been placed in liquidation. The shock of this news went all round Clydeside and beyond, but nowhere more than in Dumbarton where the effects on workers and their families were felt most keenly. "Surely not Denny's" was the reaction from many, but what was about to happen was indeed a reality, underlined by the headlines in the following day's Press: DENNY'S GO INTO LIQUIDATION - UNECONOMIC BUSINESS: HOVERCRAFT COSTS said *The Glasgow Herald*.

In meetings held in the shipyard offices the reasons for the decision were explained to the workforce, when it was said that the subsidiary company Denny Hovercraft Ltd. would be maintained as a 'going concern' in anticipation that a buyer would be found. So it was a sober group of people, which included the writer, that walked back to the Hovercraft offices. While no-one in the Hovercraft team was faced with immediate redundancy the future was at least very uncertain. The chapters that follow tell the story of how Denny's became involved in Hovercraft work and then continue through the years that included and followed that fateful announcement in July 1963. The story has many threads running through it. Two of these threads must be mentioned at the outset - the stories of Hilary Watson and Edward G. Tattersall. Hilary was one of the engineers in the Hovercraft design office, who committed himself to staying with Denny Hovercraft Ltd. until the company was ready for sale, effectively maintaining the 'going concern' almost single-handedly. The second thread is that of Edward G. Tattersall, better known as Ted. Ted was one of the engineering and scientific group within the Hovercraft Development Ltd. organisation based at Hythe on Southampton Water, requested personally by Christopher Cockerell to take on specific responsibility for the type of Hovercraft being developed by Denny's at Dumbarton. Ted was a personal and life-long friend of Christopher Cockerell, later Sir Christopher, and of course it was Cockerell who had provided a solution to the basic problem of the air cushion craft that had taxed so many minds. Cockerell coined the name 'Hovercraft'. As a tribute to him in what follows, the capital H will be used in the sections of the book produced by the writer, though this is not normal practice in what is written on the subject.

The Denny Hovercraft with their catamaran like 'sidewalls' had distinct advantages in that they were relatively quiet, had good directional control and, though not amphibious like the more glamorous types being developed by firms like Saunders-Roe, Vickers and Cushioncraft, showed considerable promise as high speed ferries. The work involved in developing this new type of marine craft, the Sidewall Hovercraft, had an infectious effect on many of those working on it, so that commitment to the project extended well beyond what might be regarded as a normal 'day job'. Thus it was not the end for Denny Hovercraft Ltd., or for the sidewall Hovercraft, when Denny's collapsed in 1963. The story went on until 1986, and still continues to this day in other parts of the world.

The writer had contact with Ted Tattersall over many years and was given a copy of the text of his paper, entitled 'The Early Days of Hovercraft Development', that he presented to the Newcomen Society in Birmingham in the year 2000, together with his permission to use the contents of the paper in any way the writer wished. It was fortunate that a copy of the paper was given to the writer since there was a disastrous fire in Ted's house and all his Hovercraft records were destroyed. Thus the writer was able to send a complete copy of the Newcomen paper back to its author. The original intention was to insert extracts from Ted's paper into the chapters that the present writer was laboriously putting together. It did not take long to realise, for a number of reasons, that this did not and would not work. So, within this little book, Ted's Newcomen lecture is presented in full, but divided into two sections. His very personal and detailed story of the early days of the Hovercraft is given in Appendix 1, with only a brief summary of the often-told and most relevant parts of the story within the main text. The second part of the Newcomen lecture is included within the main text as a chapter entitled 'The story of Hovermarine'. Probably what would have evolved was a book with joint authorship, but this could not happen due to Ted's death in March, 2011. Thus, in the text that follows the writer will refer to himself as the Author, but with full acknowledgement of the contributions from Ted Tattersall.

There were two Denny Hovercraft projects that reached completion. The first project was a 'proof of concept' craft known as D.1, the second a project intended as a fully developed commercial 'Hoverbus' and known as D.2. In the paperwork associated with these craft there is dot between the D and the project number, as in D.2. This format is retained in the text that follows though the dots were always omitted on the numbers painted on the craft. Plans were laid for building four of the D.2 craft, and these were denoted D.2-001, D.2-002 and so on.

The work at Denny's needs to be set in the context of the early 1960s when the River Clyde was lined with yards building many types of ships and with all the marine activities associated with a major trading port. In the wider world of engineering, extensive hydro-electric schemes were under construction in the Highlands and the nuclear industry held out the promise of abundant power for the future; in the aviation world Britain boasted a significant number of companies with distinguished pedigrees, building machines for world markets. Jet aircraft had been in service on the North Atlantic route for only two years. And then there was the Hovercraft. On 25th July 1959 an ungainly machine known as SR.N1 made the first crossing by Hovercraft of the English Channel from Calais to Dover. The newspapers and technical journals extrapolated the success of the SR.N1 to the construction of large ocean-going craft that would skim across the surface of the sea on their cushions of air. And trapping that air cushion below the Hovercraft is another of the main threads in the Hovercraft story.

The Author's first 'exposure' to Hovercraft was in September 1959, when the SR.N1 was demonstrated at the annual Society of British Aircraft Constructors' show at Farnborough. The Author has a clear memory of seeing this very strange machine, obviously powered by a piston engine, coming sedately along the Farnborough runway before stopping and lowering itself onto the ground in front of the spectators, at which point a group of Marines with battle gear rushed forward and climbed on board. The machine's engine then revved up, the contraption heaved itself up again and continued its sedate journey along the runway. What possible use could such a device be? The follow-up to this some months later was attendance by the Author at a Symposium on *Future Developments in Aviation*. The conference proceedings including a presentation by R. Stanton Jones of Saunders-Roe Ltd., Chief Designer on the SR.N1 Hovercraft project, on the theory, construction and development of the first full scale Hovercraft, that had crossed the English Channel and had been demonstrated at Farnborough only a few months before. It became all very interesting, and it was due to these and other influences that, in 1963, the Author joined Denny Hovercraft Ltd. as a stress engineer and where the primary task that was laid before him was involvement with the next Denny project, denoted D.3, a 130 ton craft with a welded aluminium hull.

It may be asked why someone who worked for less then nine months with Denny Hovercraft Ltd. should be writing this story. There are three reasons. The first is that no-one else seems to have done it, and the story needs to be told. The second is that the Author was able to photograph a good number of the events at Denny's Leven Shipyard in Dumbarton and elsewhere, and kept a scrap book of newspaper cuttings and odd bits of technical information. Coupled with personal memories, these items of historical value formed the core of the book, now greatly expanded from other sources such as the superb Mitchell library in Glasgow. The third reason is that after leaving Denny's the Author joined the Vickers Hovercraft Division, and having made contact with Ted Tattersall became involved in the early studies that led eventually to the formation of Hovermarine. So the Author was in the position of having links with Denny, Vickers and Hovermarine.

For many years the magazine *Flight* published a supplement called *Air Cushion Vehicles.* The Author has a set of these supplements covering the years 1963 to 1971. These were of invaluable assistance in piecing together the chapters in this book. This raises the question of how these sources should be referenced. There are many ways in which this could be done, but the Author has chosen to state the reference source at the point of quotation. Also, the Bibliography and List of References have been merged.

As the story developed, and particularly in the last Chapter, the Author often reflected on 'What might have been' if events at Denny's plus vision, support and determination in the financial world had been in greater supply. Most of the Denny design team were young, taken on and trained as 'Hovercraft Designers' by Technical Director Charles F. Morris. Working under the guidance of Morris, and with Ted Tattersall and his team at Hovercraft Development Ltd dealing with the peripheral jet technology aspect of the design, in the context of the time they did a very good job with the glass reinforced plastic D.2 craft. In a technical review of 'Fifty Years and More of Hovercraft Development' by David R. Lavis in 2011 (See References) the Denny D.2 GRP hull is listed among 'Some of the most significant developments, 1962 to 1967'. Morris's stamp is all over what had been done and with ideas for the way ahead, with plans for craft with welded aluminium structures. So 'What might have been?' and 'Why not?' From what is presented in the following chapters readers can form their own conclusions.

What the chapters do tell is of the driving force of imagination and the intense desire to bring the ideas of that imagination to successful reality, and in the case of the shipbuilding firm of William Denny and Brothers to maintain continued success in a global marketplace. These goals proved in many ways and for sometimes unexpected reasons to be elusive, due to a wide spectrum of factors that conspired and combined to make the desired outcomes so difficult to achieve. And as the Author observes later - what matters is not so much what you get right but what you get wrong. The commercial world is very unforgiving, and 'scoring nine out of ten in the assessment' is often not good enough. But he is left with admiration for those people, of which there are many, who strive to achieve things, in whatever field of endeavour, even if ultimately they do not reach the full success they sought.

Source Material and Acknowledgements

In assembling the various Chapters in this book the Author has drawn heavily on letters, newspaper cuttings, personal memories and other material from his own records; also on the indexed microfilm for *The Glasgow Herald* held in the Glasgow Mitchell library, on extracts from the *Lennox Herald* kindly obtained from Dumbarton Public Library by Craig Osborne, a volunteer archivist at the Denny Tank in Dumbarton, on extracts from newspapers local to Blackpool sent by Blackpool Public Library, and on several reports from the Kingston, Jamaica, paper *The Gleaner*. Technical Journal and book references are listed in the References and Bibliography section following Chapter 13.

Over half of the photographs and illustrations in the book are by the Author. Most of the Author's oldest photographs are from 35mm Kodachrome transparencies taken with a Leica 3g camera , but some are single frames extracted by the Author's friend Stephen Kunz from the ciné film 'Denny Hovercraft' (See Appendix 2). Thanks are also extended to another friend, aviation historian Peter Berry, for the picture in Chapter 3 of SR.N1 hovering over the Farnborough runway in 1959. Peter was one of the airfield controllers at the time. Thanks are also due to John Brennan who made a special visit to the Discovery Museum in Newcastle to photograph the *Turbinia*. A special appreciation is due to Robin Denny for extending the Author's knowledge on a number of Denny innovations in a very personal way and for breaking the 'writer's block' that troubled the Author for a time. In addition to his mention above, naval architect Craig Osborne has been of great assistance and generous with his encyclopaedic knowledge of things maritime, and of Denny's in particular. During the writing of this book, over a very extended period, the staff of the Scottish Maritime Museum, under Anne Hoben at the Denny Tank in Dumbarton, have been very patient and helpful.

Attempts were made to find former employees of Denny Hovercraft Ltd., but with almost no success until contact was made with Hugh Orr, the former Manager of the Hovercraft company, via his brother John. Hugh Orr helped with a number of matters of fact and with providing permission to use his photographs from his Hovercraft years at Denny's. Since then Hugh has transferred his pictures and copyright interest to the Scottish Maritime Museum. In Chapters 4, 6 and 10 there are pictures based on photographs given to the Author in 1963 by members of the DHL design team. This is as close as the Author can get to attribution for these.

Special thanks are due to Warwick Jacobs, a Trustee of the Hovercraft Museum Trust at Lee-on-the-Solent, for providing access to a considerable number of pictures from the Hovercraft Museum archive. This archive includes material from private individuals and organisations like Westland/Saunders-Roe and Vickers, as well as Hovercraft Development Limited. The copyright attribution for these is the Hovercraft Museum Trust. The pictures to which this applies are of SR.N3, SR.N5, VA-1, VA-2 and VA-3 in Chapter 1; the D.3 model in Chapter 5; *Denny Enterprise* at sea, *Humming Bird* being loaded onto the freighter at Liverpool docks, D.2-003 at Fleetwood and D.2-002 off Florida in Chapter 11. Also in Chapter 11 is the picture of the Hon. Robert Lightbourne going aboard *Humming Bird* at Kingston, Jamaica; the copyright for this picture is held by the Jamaican paper *The Daily Gleaner*. Also in Chapter 11, the photograph of D.2-003 on the Thames in 1972 was taken by Alan Blunden, who has asked that it is attributed 'Copyright Fast Ferry International'.

The sectional drawings of D.2 in Chapter 4 are from the original Denny General Arrangement drawing held in the archive of the Scottish Maritime Museum at Irvine. The Hovermarine illustrations are mainly from material supplied to the Author by Ted Tattersall.

Huge thanks are due to Ken Pemberton of the *Hovermail Collectors Club* and for 25 years Editor of the club magazine *Slipstream*. Ken went to great lengths digging out information relating to the obscure later years in the history of the Denny D.2s 002 and 003. Without Ken's help these later years would have been even more obscure! As a follow on to this, thanks are also due to Dave Galka, editor of the Hoverclub of America publication *Hovernews*, for going through his archives to find the letter from Dennis Daly telling a little of the adventures of Denny Hovercraft D.2-002 in America.

Perhaps somewhat belatedly in this record of assistance given to the Author, particular thanks are given warmly to Dave Lacey, a long-standing colleague of the Author on the committee of the Prestwick Branch of the Royal Aeronautical Society. Dave proof read an earlier version of the book, paying great attention to detail in his usual meticulous way. Quite a few items were added to the book after that, so any errors are totally attributable to the Author, who did not have the heart to ask Dave to go through it again!

It was very generous of Professor Dugald Cameron to take time to write the Foreword to this book at a time when he was particularly busy preparing for the next exhibition of his aviation paintings.

Finally the Author must express his appreciation of the great patience and support shown by his wife Elizabeth. Without this help it is probable that the work in assembling this book would never have reached the level of completion it did - there really is no end to the kinds of stories it contains since new items of information kept and still keep emerging.

Chapter 1

Why "Hovercraft"?

Seamen have long known that the performance of a ship would depend on many factors, including the shape or form of the hull, and the smoothness of the hull below the water. Careening was standard practice, involving beaching or heaving a vessel down on one side by heavy tackles so that the keel came above the surface of the water, allowing marine growths to be scraped from the exposed area of the hull. The intuitive understanding that shipbuilders and seamen had of these matters was put on a scientific basis by the work of William Froude, who in 1861 read his first paper on the rolling of ships before the Institution of Naval Architects, leading to his participation in 1868 in a committee studying naval design. His proposals to the Admiralty for the construction of a ship-model testing tank were accepted in 1870 and this was duly built near his home in Torquay. This, the first ship-model testing tank in the world, gave Britain a very significant advantage in ship design and other tanks were built, the first commercial ship-model experiment tank being constructed and brought into operation at the Denny yard in Dumbarton in 1883.

A memorial plaque to William Froude, who died in 1879, was mounted on the external wall of the office and workshop building at the end of the Denny tank, where it can still be seen by the general public and visitors to the tank installation, now a part of the Scottish Maritime Museum. Testing scale models of proposed ships in the way devised by Froude has remained standard practice to the present day.

Froude's work allowed the question of hull resistance to be divided into two components that could be examined and assessed separately - resistance due to wave making and resistance due to friction between the hull and the water. The model testing tank opened the way to reducing the wave-making drag of ships' hulls. One obvious response to the skin friction question was lubrication, but how was this to be done?

The journal *Air-Cushion Vehicles* in its June 1964 issue published an article describing the work of John Isaac Thorneycroft, later Sir John, and quoting from a patent granted to him in 1877: "According to my Invention, in order to reduce the friction of a vessel when travelling on the water I interpose a layer or body of air between the bottom of the vessel and the surface of the water, which air I confine within a cavity of the bottom of the vessel so that the air shall be carried along with the vessel over the surface of the water ...". Thorneycroft was at that time engaged in the design of a small vessel and potential torpedo boat, H.M.S. *Lightning*, and models with and without cavities in the bottom of the hull were made for testing. Mixed results were obtained, but enough to lead Thorneycroft to lay down some basic principles that would need to be followed if future progress was to be made. It should be noted that this work by Thorneycroft was in 1873, around about the same time that William Froude's tank began producing test results.

A further article in *Air-Cushion Vehicles* (December 1963) described Mr. Schroeder's Patent of

1906, complete with an artist's impression that showed a craft with a system for lifting the craft by air and for propelling it by air jets. Another article, published in November and entitled 'Sam Saunders - the S in SR.N' described the ideas of Saunders dating from about 1909 involving the use of air below a vessel to reduce drag and to give passengers a more comfortable ride. In his lecture to the Newcomen Society in Birmingham in the year 2000, Ted Tattersall described some model work done by William Froude, in anticipation that air lubrication would reduce ship resistance. " ... he drilled holes in the bottom through which he could feed air under pressure. To his consternation the model resistance increased and as a result he never pursued this line of investigation". In fact, these are only a few of the many proposals made over many years. Clearly, attractive as the idea was of reducing hull resistance by lubrication with air injected below waterline level, the practical application of the principle was not going to be easy (in fact research on the application to typical merchant vessels goes on to the present day).

The invention offering a solution that could work well emerged in the 1950s from the Norfolk Broads boatyard of Christopher Cockerell. His experiments led him to conclude that what was needed was a space or cavity under his craft and filled with air - a plenum - rather than a film of air. This was a similar conclusion to that reached by Thorneycroft. A detailed and personal record of how Cockerell created his engineered solution to the problem of air lubrication was recounted by Ted Tattersall in his Newcomen lecture, *The Early Days of Hovercraft Development*. Ted was a close friend of Christopher Cockerell and his very personal record of these early days is given in full in Appendix 1. The purpose of what follows here is to give enough of the story to explain the developments that led to William Denny and Brothers becoming involved in the development of air cushion craft.

Cockerell's early experiments were with a punt to which he had attached side keels and transverse sprung doors at the front and back, thus creating a space underneath, a plenum, which could contain the slightly pressurised air cushion. The idea of holding the doors on springs was to allow them to respond to waves and to minimise impact. Tests soon showed that the air cushion had a very beneficial effect on the resistance experienced by the punt, but that the rigid doors, even though sprung, were buffeted unacceptably. Something much more flexible was required. Further experiments led Cockerell to the idea of using air jets, coming from transverse slots between the side keels, to contain the air cushion.

A further development led to an idea for a different form of air cushion craft, one with air jets all round its periphery. Cockerell made the initial test of this concept when he conducted his classic experiment with two tin cans, one within the other, a hand held air blower and kitchen scales, as illustrated in the diagram. This proved that the uplift created by the can arrangement was significantly greater than that produced by the air blower alone.

Further tests with a self-propelled model built using model aeroplane techniques proved the concept and demonstrated that a fully amphibious craft could be developed. Thus, from very early on, two distinct types

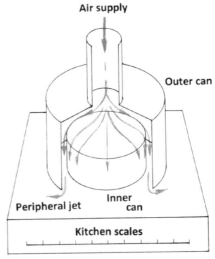

of craft were envisaged, one with catamaran-like side keels (later called sidewalls) and limited to operation on water, and one that could operate on water or land and possibly on many other surfaces, the so-called peripheral craft. Cockerel coined the word 'Hovercraft' to describe air-cushion vehicles employing his air jet principle for containment of the air cushion, either partly as with the sidewall type or all round the craft periphery.

For a time he was faced with the problem of funding, and of finding companies that would be interested in developing his invention. Eventually, after a period of secrecy when the Ministry of Defence was looking into his ideas, Cockerell became free to approach the National Research and Development Corporation - NRDC. NRDC had been established by the British Government after World War 2, initially to exploit commercially the many ideas that had been developed during the war. The concept was that NRDC would hold the necessary patents, possibly assist with 'seed-corn' funding, and earn royalties as private companies became licensed to use the patents and to sell the products developed. In due course, NRDC formed Hovercraft Development Ltd. (HDL), a research company that would take ownership of Cockerell's patents and would have Cockerell as Managing Director. Any firm wishing to use the Hovercraft patents would have to obtain a licence from HDL. Already working with Cockerell prior to the formation of HDL, Ted Tattersall became one of HDL's first employees.

Model of SR.N1

The experimental SR.N1 Hovercraft, designed and built by Saunders-Roe just before it became a Division within the Westland Aircraft Group, proved the amphibious Hovercraft concept at full scale with a crossing of the English Channel on 25th July 1959, the 50th anniversary of Bleriot's crossing in 1909.

This work gave Saunders-Roe a head start in the Hovercraft business, with studies and project design work proceeding on other craft that became the SR.N2 and SR.N3, the big cross-channel SR.N4, and the much smaller but still capable SR.N5 and SR.N6.

SR.N2 model at the 1960 Farnborough Air Show

SR.N5 - launched April 1964

SR.N3- launched December 1963. And an outline sketch of the projected SR.N4 that first emerged from the builder's hangar at Cowes in October 1967.

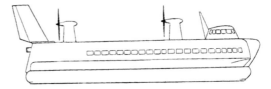

Vickers-Armstrong also became interested, leading to the formation of its Hovercraft Division at its South Marston works near Swindon. Vickers built its VA-1, VA-2 and VA-3. VA-1 was very much a learning exercise, VA-2 was used primarily for research and VA-3 became the first Hovercraft to operate a commercial service, across the Dee estuary between Rhyl in North Wales and Wallasey near Liverpool, for a short period during the summer of 1962.

VA-1 upper left,

VA-2 upper right,

and VA-3 in British United Airways livery during the pioneering operation between Rhyl and Wallasey.

Joined by J. Samuel White, a Cowes, Isle of Wight, shipbuilder, these three were the initial members of the Hovercraft 'Club'. The licence held by Samuel White restricted the company to amphibious craft with a maximum of 20 seats while Westland and Vickers were unrestricted. In his Newcomen lecture Ted described how he was excited by the possibilities offered by the amphibious craft, and was disappointed when Cockerell asked him to "champion" the sidewall non-amphibious type. Quoting from his lecture, and referring to the sidewall Hovercraft: "Soon I proved at least that such a craft could out-perform high speed displacement craft. Based on this and the limited amount of testing that was being undertaken at the Cockerell's new family home (The White Cottage), NRDC and HDL contacted William Denny's of Dumbarton, who at that time were famous for their ferry boat and river boat designs. What's more, they were armed with a test tank. Denny's soon became licensees to the HDL patents and I found myself commuting quite frequently between the Isle of Wight and the Clyde".

It has been suggested to the Author that NRDC and HDL may have approached a number of firms with the proposal to become involved in the commercial development of the sidewall Hovercraft. While this may have been so, it would have been surprising if William Denny and Brothers had not emerged quickly as front runners. If we go back first of all to mid-1958 when Saunders-Roe were carrying out the initial design studies that led to the construction of SR.N1, and then to the years immediately following, it could be said that the development of projects for larger commercial craft of the amphibious type was proceeding well, and with a feeling of urgency. But what about the sidewall type that had been the basis of some of Cockerell's original experiments? This was an avenue that Cockerell was been keen to explore, with the possibility of using different technologies from the aircraft approach employed on the more weight sensitive amphibious types with their complete peripheral jet arrangement. And while it might be questioned whether the amphibious types were ships or aircraft or a mixture of both, the sidewall type was definitely a ship. So the preferred partner and licensee of the patents held by HDL would be a ship builder, and Denny's with their long record of enterprise, excellence, innovation and market knowledge would have stood out. Another factor that was an advantage to Denny's was easy access to the Firth of Clyde and good trials areas complete with measured miles. The nearest was on the sheltered and quiet waters of the Gareloch, only about 15 miles by water from Denny's Leven shipyard.

When William Denny and Brothers joined Saunders-Roe/Westlands and Vickers in the Hovercraft 'Club' these 'big three' became engaged in the design of large craft. Years before, when Cockerell was carrying out his classic experiments with his tin cans and hand-held air blower he realised that the power requirement for the air jet cushion system was proportional to the length around the craft circumference, but that the carrying capacity of the craft was proportional the craft's plan area, which would be proportional to the square of the length of the craft's circumference (If we imagine a craft with a circular planform and diameter D, the length round the periphery is πD and the plan area is $\pi D^2/4$). This basic piece of mathematics, while simplistic, indicated clearly that there was a definite advantage in building craft as large as knowledge and economics allowed. It was also the case that a large craft would be likely to give passengers a smoother ride than a small craft. The size factor alone would not have been a problem to a shipyard like Denny's. The three 'large craft studies' were the Westland SR.N4, the Vickers VA-4 and the Denny D.3. The SR.N4, designed and built by Westland's Saunders-Roe Division, was the only one of the three that went beyond the paper and model stage. Six of the 200 ton SR.N4s were built, serving on the English Channel ferry routes until the last was withdrawn in October 2000, after 32 years of operation carrying passengers and cars since the first scheduled crossing in June 1968.

Chapter 2

William Denny and Brothers - a record of Enterprise and Innovation

In any history of William Denny and Brothers, however brief, there are always certain selected projects that are mentioned, and often little is said about the people who were associated with the projects. For most of its existence Denny's was very much a family firm involving several generations and many remarkable people, from within and also from outside the family. The Author hopes that the short account that follows will be sufficient to do justice to this enterprising and innovative company without overburdening the reader with detail.

The early history of William Denny and Brothers, up to 1904, is described by Captain James Williamson in his classic book 'Clyde Passenger Steamers from 1812 to 1901'. It is recounted that the origin of the firm lay in the early 1800s when William Denny, a well regarded shipbuilder, occupied ground at what was known as the Woodyard on the west side of the river Leven at Dumbarton. The vessels built were described as being of a "humble character, consisting, for the most part, of small wooden coasting smacks, schooners and the like". But among them was the little paddle steamer *Marjory* that was built in 1814 and found its way south to become London's first passenger steamboat in 1815, and to cross the Channel. *Marjory* was built only two years after Henry Bell's steamboat *Comet* went into service on the Clyde and heralded the era of steam navigation in Europe.

William Denny had eleven children, a number of whom showed great talent in shipbuilding. Three,

William, Alexander and Peter, formed a partnership as marine architects in Glasgow under the name 'Denny Brothers'. After a few years the partnership was dissolved and a new firm formed in 1849 by William, Peter and James Denny, with the name 'William Denny and Brothers', the name still retained by the company when it was approached by NRDC and HDL in 1959 to become involved in the development of the Hovercraft. William Denny, the senior partner and "ruling spirit" in the firm died in 1854 at an early age, leaving Peter and James to carry on as best they could. Peter Denny's feelings are described in his own words: "A great calamity to me took place in the death of my brother William aged 39. I was so depressed and disheartened that I needed all the encouragement of my friends to induce me to carry on the business, being so imperfectly qualified as to the technical and practical work, and having the necessity of the commercial department wholly upon myself". Peter Denny did carry on, and to such good effect that, after his death in 1895, the citizens of Dumbarton erected a statue to his memory and to celebrate his achievements, outside the new municipal building in Dumbarton.

In 1865 Peter Denny formed a partnership with T.D. Findlay to create the Irrawaddy Flotilla Company. A very large number of the Company ships, at least 300 and possibly most of the whole fleet of 600, were designed and built in Dumbarton specifically to suit the shallow waters of the Irrawaddy. The following two quotations are from the web site www.irrawaddyflotilla.com: "They became the lifeblood of the nation's prosperity, ensuring trade up and down the great rivers, and aiding Burma's transformation into the rice-bowl of Asia". And who could resist a bit of Kipling? "Come you back to Mandalay, where the old Flotilla lay: Can't you 'ear their paddles chunkin' from Rangoon to Mandalay?"

In 1869 a clipper ship was being built on the banks of the Leven by the firm of Scott and Linton. Money ran out and the contract to complete the vessel was taken over by William Denny and Brothers. The ship became famous as the renowned *Cutty Sark*, still preserved at Greenwich on the Thames, now extensively repaired after a disastrous fire. Though Denny or Denny's, as the company was commonly known, had completed a sailing ship, the interest and expertise of the company lay almost entirely in iron ships with steam engines.

Following the construction of Froude's experiment tank at Torquay in 1871, the Denny company followed suit by building at Dumbarton, and bringing into operation on 21st February 1883, the first commercial ship-model testing tank in the world, now preserved and still functional as part of the Scottish Maritime Museum. The effectiveness of this foresighted action by the company can be judged by quoting the words of Captain James Williamson, referring to the Denny yard: "One of the most interesting features is the experimental tank, constructed upon the lines of that of the late William Froude at Torquay. Its value to the firm in making close calculations of the H.P. required in propelling steam vessels of all classes can hardly be over-estimated, and the large expenditure involved in its formation, maintenance, and working, has been amply repaid by the success which has attended its use". By the time the experiment tank was built the Denny yard extended from the Leven shipyard to the foot of Dumbarton Castle rock.

Peter Denny had a number of children, several of whom joined him in the firm when they reached a suitable age. First was William in 1868, followed by John and nephew James in 1881, then Peter and Archibald in 1883, and later Leslie in 1895. Despite having described himself as "so imperfectly qualified as to the technical and practical work" and saying that he was burdened by "the necessity of the commercial department wholly upon myself", when he and James were left to run the business in 1854, Peter Denny made such a success of what he did and became so respected that he was appointed (1871) to a government Committee on Designs for Ships of War and to a Royal Commission (1873-1874) to enquire into the causes of the loss of life and property at sea. He received honours from the Spanish and Portuguese governments, and an LL.D from the University of Glasgow, and found time to contribute to the municipal life of Dumbarton, including filling the position of Provost. He suffered a shock that had a permanent effect on his health when his eldest son William died in 1887. It had been William who had encouraged the partners in the firm to build the ship-model testing tank and it was William who had introduced progressive speed trials over a measured mile.

Archibald Denny (1860 - 1936) had a distinguished career and is credited with his involvement with developing the experiment tank and as a partner in charge of technical developments at the shipyard. He was awarded an LL.D. by the University of Glasgow in 1911 and became Sir Archibald, 1st Baronet Denny in 1913, in recognition of "his close association with Denny's international reputation for innovation and high quality ship design". He was also a technical consultant to various Government departments and served on many industry committees and commissions involved in setting and investigating technical standards in the industry. According to information provided by the Scottish Maritime Museum, the first ship model tested in the tank in 1883 was of *Rotomahana*. A few years previously, in 1877, the British Admiralty had built the *Iris* and the *Mercury* using steel instead of wrought iron. The Denny Company tried working with this new material on lightweight vessels for the Irrawaddy Flotilla Company before using it to construct the *Rotomahana*, making this ship the first ocean-going vessel built of steel.

In 1888, ship no. 386, the paddle steamer *Princess Henriette* with its speed of 20.5 knots became the fastest commercial vessel in the world. Only naval torpedo boats went faster.

The vessel that changed everything in the field of ship propulsion was the *Turbinia*, built at Wallsend on Tyne and launched in 1894 to test Charles Parsons' new form of marine propulsion machinery, the steam turbine. *Turbinia* was demonstrated in the most dramatic way when she raced round the fleet during Queen Victoria's Diamond Jubilee Naval Review off Portsmouth in 1897. This pioneering vessel is preserved in the Discovery Museum in Newcastle Upon Tyne. To absorb the power from her steam turbines, *Turbinia* was tested with up to nine propellers on three shafts, as displayed in the museum.

The impressive performance of Parsons' turbines, demonstrated by *Turbinia*, led to another of Denny's technical achievements - the construction of the first commercial vessel to be powered by steam turbines, summed up by James Williamson as "playing a notable part in the introduction of this type of machinery which is likely to revolutionise the engineering world in the twentieth century hardly less than James Watt's invention of the separate condenser did in the nineteenth". This vessel was not 'made to order' in the usual way. Very early in 1901 it was announced that a syndicate had been formed to build a turbine steamer. The firms making up the 'Turbine Syndicate' were William Denny and Brothers Ltd., Parsons Marine Steam Turbine Co. Ltd. of Wallsend-on-Tyne and John Williamson and Co. of Glasgow. Thus Denny's and the other members of the syndicate had to obtain and provide the finance to build the new ship; Denny's built the vessel and the engines were provided by Parsons. Captain John Williamson became the Managing Director of the syndicate (He was the brother of James Williamson, the author of 'Clyde Passenger Steamers from 1812 to 1901'). The T.S.S. *King Edward* went into regular service in July 1901, only about six months after the laying of the vessel's keel! She was an immediate success.

The picture shows the model of the *King Edward* displayed as it was in Kelvingrove Museum in Glasgow in 1972; it is now displayed in Glasgow's new Riverside Museum. It is just possible to see in the picture that the model has five propellers, two on each of the wing shafts and one on the centre shaft, as tried out on Parsons' experimental vessel *Turbinia*. It was found that a better performance was obtained with three propellers, one on each shaft, and *King Edward* operated for the rest of her life as a triple screw turbine steamer. During her long and successful operational career *King Edward* even ventured far from her home waters of the Firth of Clyde. Shortly after the Armistice that ended WW1, when the British Government made an ill-considered and abortive attempt to interfere in Russia on the side of the White Army against the Red, the *King Edward* made a voyage to Archangel, even though she was certainly not designed for the sea and weather conditions that could be experienced around the North Cape or off the coast of Norway. The *King Edward* was in operation for fifty one years, finally being retired in 1952.

The Author has to make an admission here. Around 1950 he travelled to Glasgow with a school friend, intending to sail down-river to Dunoon on the big, comfortable, Denny built *Queen Mary II* (the picture shows *Queen Mary II* passing John Brown's yard at Clydebank), and was disappointed when confronted with an ancient looking turbine steamer for the journey to Dunoon. At

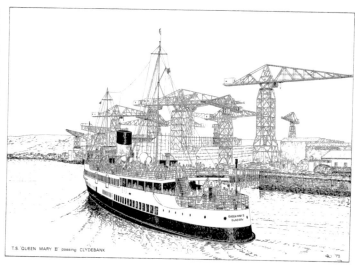

T.S. 'QUEEN MARY II' passing CLYDEBANK

that time the views along the river were awe-inspiring - mile after mile of quays and docks lined with ships being fitted out or loading and unloading, and slipway after slipway with ships in various stages of construction. It was some time later that realisation dawned on the Author of the significance of that "ancient looking turbine steamer", *King Edward*. Shame on him!!

If the reader will forgive just a little more reminiscing: the Author remembers standing on the edge of Dunoon pier looking down at one of the propellers on a turbine steamer, glinting and clearly visible under the water. The clanging of the bells on the bridge telegraph was followed immediately by the propeller spinning into action, creating a close pitched spiral of bubbles from the tip of each blade. As the steamer began to move ahead and speed built up, the pitch of the bubble helix quickly increased before being lost to sight. Try making an observation like this in the modern Health and Safety age!

One of the steam turbines from the *King Edward* is preserved by the Scottish Maritime Museum (and a second at the Glasgow Riverside Museum), where there is also a model of the Denny-Mumford helicopter. With the examples of technical innovation previously described it should not be surprising that the company became involved in aviation. The Tank Superintendent E.R. Mumford experimented with his design of a helicopter in the 1905 - 1914 period, using his knowledge of ship propellers, judging by the appearance of the rotors. Unfortunately, the six rotor machine - it was quite large - was destroyed in a gale before complete testing could be carried out. There are photographs of this machine and the model in the Scottish Maritime Museum merits examination. It is worth noting that an advantage of the six rotor arrangement was that, since three rotors rotated in one direction and three in the opposite, the rotor torques almost balanced, avoiding the problems of asymmetry that were encountered later in the design of single rotor helicopters.

Another innovative vessel was the *King George V*, powered by high pressure steam turbines; but possibly one of the most successful innovations was the Denny-Brown ship stabiliser that

significantly reduced the rolling motion of a vessel at sea. At this point the Author must express his appreciation of the letters received from Robin D.L. Denny and for the detailed information contained in the Museum booklet on the Denny Tank. Very briefly, the first practical application of fin stabilisers for ships was achieved by Mitsubishi in Japan in the 1920-1932 period. In the U.K., the Edinburgh firm of Brown Brothers was interested in the device and a partner was needed to develop its use. As Mr. Robin Denny said in one of his letters, "it seems to have been normal practice to hawk an idea around every yard that might be interested. The Brown Brothers engineer (Probably William Wallace: Author.) tried everyone on the Clyde to take up his stabilisers. It was only on his second visit that my uncle, Edward Denny, finally agreed". The two firms took out a licence for the Japanese design in 1933, and from this time onwards the Denny-Brown ship stabiliser became very famous and a requirement for many types of ship. The Royal Navy had them fitted to warships to provide more stable gunnery platforms, and commercial ships had them fitted to give passengers a more comfortable passage. The story is told that the Cunard Company decided, after WW2, not to have them fitted to the liner *Queen Mary* during her post-war refit because she was too old. This decision had to be reversed later because of passenger complaints about the motion of the ship in the North Atlantic. A working demonstration model of a Brown of Edinburgh ship stabiliser, a later version of the Denny-Brown, is on display at the Scottish Maritime Museum in Irvine. The obvious and essential features of the invention were the two (or more) fins that protruded from either side of a ship and were operated like control surfaces on the wings of an aeroplane to counteract the wave-induced motion of the vessel. To avoid damage, when docking for instance, the fin installation could be designed so that the fins could be retracted to within the profile of the hull. Actuators within the hull were operated by a control system that used gyroscopes to sense ship motion and apply the appropriate movement of the fins at the correct stage in the rolling motion of the ship. Tests on the system were conducted in the experiment tank at Dumbarton. Brown Brothers were taken over by Vickers in the late 1980s before being purchased by Rolls-Royce in 1999. Rolls-Royce has a factory at Dalgety Bay in Fife, manufacturing ship stabilisers and steering gear.

Sir Archibald Denny's first son was Maurice (1886 - 1955) who became the second Baronet on the death of his father in 1936. Maurice was educated at Tonbridge School in England, in Switzerland and in Germany and at the Massachusetts Institute of Technology in Boston, USA - the famous M.I.T. He was Chairman of Denny's from 1922 to 1952 and President from 1953. It has been stated that he enhanced the reputation of William Denny and Brothers for all classes of work. His competence and the breadth of his interests can be judged by the fact that, in addition to being on the Boards of various companies with financial, shipping and a wide range of engineering interests, he became the first Chairman of the Air Registration Board (The ARB for short). The very early days of aviation in the U.K. had been largely a free-for-all, with the possible exception of licensing of pilots by the Royal Aero Club. Ensuring that the machines themselves were airworthy became the province of the Air Ministry and continued to be so until April 1st, 1937, when the Air Registration Board began operation and took on the airworthiness aspects of civil aircraft, leaving the Air Ministry to continue dealing with military aircraft. A report on the first annual dinner held by the new Air Registration Board appeared in the journal *Flight* dated February 10, 1938. And in the copy of *Flight* dated July 26, 1945, there is a report of a speech by Sir Maurice, still in his position as Chairman, with a list of members of Council that included famous names in the aviation world like Sir Frederick Handley Page, and Sir Roy Dobson of Avro and the Hawker Siddeley Group. His wide range of technical competence is further illustrated by his involvement from 1944 with the British Shipbuilding Research Association, of which he was a member and later Chairman.

Alan Sherry's book *The Blackburn: Dumbarton's Aircraft Factory* tells the story of how Sir Maurice became introduced to Robert Blackburn, leading in 1937 to the creation of the Blackburn Aircraft Factory adjacent to the Denny yard and only separated from it by Castle Road. Robert Blackburn was one of the very early aviation pioneers in the UK, building his first aeroplane, the *Blackburn First Monoplane* in 1909 and creating a distinguished company that went on to build a wide range of aircraft types in considerable numbers. The date 1937, with the threat of another war looming, indicates part of the reason for setting up the aircraft factory. The other part was Sir Maurice's concern to diversify industry in Dumbarton, and, of course, his interest in and knowledge of aviation.

The Dumbarton aircraft factory carried out manufacturing and other work on a number of aircraft types, and had its own design organisation, but is probably best remembered for producing Sunderland flying boats during WW2. In 1954, the Author, in the company of other young apprentices from Scottish Aviation at Prestwick, visited the factory and saw fuselage sections for Bristol Britannia airliners being built. The factory doors closed in 1961, though the rundown was virtually complete by the middle of 1960. The existence of aircraft construction skills could have been very relevant to the Hovercraft work that was about to start at the Denny yard just across the road.

In a letter to the Author in 2012, Mr. Robin Denny noted that Sir Maurice was instrumental in fitting four jet engines to the hull of the *Lucy Ashton*. Built by T.B. Seath of Rutherglen in 1888 and being scheduled for scrapping in 1950, the opportunity was taken by the British Shipbuilding Research Association (BSRA) to use the old paddler for full-scale hull resistance measurements, using a method that had only become possible following the development of the jet engine. At the Denny yard, *Lucy*'s paddles were removed and a transverse structure fitted to mount four Rolls-Royce *Derwent* engines, and also to fit 'flaps' that could be lowered into the water when necessary to slow the ship. Otherwise she had no brakes! The thrust of the four jet engines was easily measured and there was none of the interference with the hull performance that would have occurred with any form of water driven propulsion. The full scale resistance data could then be compared with predictions based on tank test data. The results from this work were published progressively in the Transactions of the Royal Institution of Naval Architects from 1951 onwards. Also, round about 1950, studies were conducted by Denny's into the design of a hydrofoil boat capable of 52 knots.

With this sort of shipbuilding pedigree it should not be surprising that the Denny Company became involved in Hovercraft work, through the agreement in 1960 for the joint development programme entered into with Hovercraft Development Limited, the wholly owned subsidiary of the National Research Development Corporation. However, Ted Tattersall's remark had been about the firm being "famous for their ferry boat and river boat designs". In the years immediately prior to becoming involved in Hovercraft development, say from 1957 onwards, the yard built ships like the *Bardic Ferry* and *Ionic Ferry*, cross-channel passenger, car and container motor vessels for the Atlantic S N Co. Three newsprint carriers were built for the Bowater S.S. Co.: the *Nicholas Bowater, Gladys Bowater* and *Phyllis Bowater.* Single screw turbine engine cargo steamers were

built for the Lyle Shipping Co.: the *Cape Sable* and *Cape Wrath*. In 1961, a twin-screw diesel-electric car, passenger and train cross-channel ship, the *Aramoana*, was launched for New Zealand Railways. These few examples, and what has been said before, give a clear indication of the well-founded and all-round competence in all the departments making up the ship building firm of William Denny and Brothers.

The entrance to the Denny Experiment Tank Museum at Dumbarton, part of the Scottish Maritime Museum.

Chapter 3

The Basic Ideas behind the Original Hovercraft

In Chapter 1 it has been recounted how the National Research Development Corporation became involved in the Hovercraft story. It was clear that Christopher Cockerell's ideas had promise, but would they work on a full-size craft? In September 1958 Saunders-Roe made a proposal to the National Research Development Corporation (NRDC). for the design of a manned craft. The proposal was accepted and detailed design work began the following month. After the trials and tribulations that are a normal feature of the design process, SR.N1 hovered in the spring of 1959 and in July of that year crossed the English Channel on the 50th anniversary of Bleriot's epic flight.

The development of the Hovercraft as we know it today has depended on two primary inventions - Cockerell's concept of the peripheral air jet, and the development of the flexible skirt. The flexible skirt will be discussed in a later chapter. It was the concept of the peripheral jet, sometimes called the momentum curtain, that turned the idea of the air lubricated boat from dream to reality. If we look at the picture of the Saunders-Roe SR.N1 at the 1959 Society of British Aircraft Constructors show we can see that it is no magic carpet, though it is certainly hovering a small distance above the Farnborough runway.

The force that is holding SR.N1 above the ground is the pressure of the air in the 'cushion' trapped between the ground and the bottom of the craft, and contained round the edges of the craft by Christopher Cockerell's invention - the momentum curtain formed by the peripheral jet arrangement. The only visible sign of this is the small cloud of dust from the runway.

The way in which the peripheral jet system worked on SR.N1 was that, first of all, air was drawn into the white painted 'chimney' by a fan driven through a gear box by an aircraft engine, a 450 h.p. Alvis Leonides. This air was blown into a space within the craft known as a plenum, which ducted the air to a two inch wide slot going all the way round the outer edge of the craft, and also an inner slot. These 'slots' were shaped so that they formed continuous annular nozzles directing the air downwards and inwards at an angle of about 45°. When the engine was started up with SR.N1 sitting on the ground, air was blown from these nozzles and forced underneath the craft until the pressure of the air on the bottom surface was sufficient to lift the craft free of the ground. The height to which the craft rose depended on the power delivered by the engine and the air flow delivered by the fan - more power and air flow giving greater height, with the annular jet system pressurising the 'cushion', and the cushion pressure forcing the annular air jets to turn outwards. Simple though this system was in principle, the people at Saunders-Roe found by means of tests on working models and by mathematical analysis that the SR.N1 could be unstable, so that it could tip over until an edge of the craft came in contact with the ground. This was discovered during the construction phase of SR.N1. The solution was to add the second row of peripheral jets, which is why the craft ended up with a double row.

Another issue the designers of SR.N1 had to deal with was how to propel the craft. If funds had allowed, a separate engine driving an airscrew, or even a small jet engine, might have been simple solution. Since funds were tight the decision was to use some of the air flow developed by the fan and to divert it through ducts along the sides of the craft to produce forward or rearward acting thrusts as required. In addition to having gate valves, internal shutters to direct the air rearwards giving forward thrust, or forwards giving reverse thrust, the ducts also had control vanes at the exits. By these means the designers had solved the problems of propulsion and directional control. Having said this, the propulsion of SR.N1 was a compromise solution and not one the designers would have preferred to follow, with the efficiency of the ducted propulsion being as low as 50%. This matter of propelling a hovercraft begs the question of what are the forces that the propulsion system must overcome?

Anyone who has ridden a bicycle will know how hard it is to cycle into the wind compared with cycling with the wind coming from behind. It takes effort to push a body through the air and it is also known that the effort required can be reduced by streamlining the body. This force resisting motion and exerted by the air is called aerodynamic drag. SR.N1 was certainly not streamlined, but its primary function was to investigate what could be done using Cockerell's ideas; so at this early stage aerodynamic drag was of secondary importance.

Another form of drag affecting SR.N1 is less obvious. This time, instead of asking the reader to imagine riding a bicycle the author will ask the reader to imagine being in a car that is driven at speed into a long puddle of water about an inch or two deep. Apart from seeing the spray going everywhere, the occupants of the car will get a strong feeling of braking, without the driver touching the car brakes. Something similar to this happens to a hovercraft even when it is being flown over dry land. This resistance to motion is known as momentum drag. It arises because, as SR.N1 speeds along, it draws air into its 'chimney' and briefly carries this air along within the craft plenum and ducting until it is expelled in all directions around the craft periphery. Before being expelled the air has to be accelerated to have the same mean speed as the craft, which results in the so-called momentum drag. The more air that has to be drawn in to maintain the air cushion the higher the momentum drag, and the faster the craft travels the higher the momentum drag. Thus, to minimise momentum drag it is desirable to supply as little air as possible to the air cushion, which is at odds with producing the necessary 'hover height', the distance from the bottom of the craft to the ground.

From quite early on, Cockerell had considered ways of reducing the power requirement of his air jet system but at this period the problem remained unsolved. The technology of the flexible skirt lay in the future. One option that was already available for reducing the fan power was to design a craft with two hulls in a catamaran arrangement, so that Cockerell's 'peripheral jets' were only needed at the front and rear. This will be discussed later, when William Denny and Brothers become involved. For the present we shall follow the SR.N1 story.

One very attractive feature of a Hovercraft like SR.N1 was that it could travel over land or sea. Operating over water introduces additional forms of 'drag'.

As this is being written in 2013 there are frequent references in the media to alternative sources of energy, with 'wave energy' machines being designed to extract energy from the motion of the waves. Having asked the reader to imagine being on a bicycle and in a car, the author's next request is to imagine being on a ship, looking over the side at the waves created by the ship. These waves contain energy, so what is the source of this energy? The answer to that is the engine of the ship, which turns the propeller and pushes the ship forward, the hull displacing water as it goes and creating waves. The thrust of the propeller has to overcome the resistance or drag of the water on the ship's hull. Surely a Hovercraft that does not touch the surface of the sea cannot create waves and cannot experience drag due to making waves! The short answer is that it does.

When SR.N1 was stationary over smooth water and on its cushion, the cushion pressure of around 19 pounds per square foot (lb/ft^2) above atmospheric pressure caused a depression of about 3½ inches (9 cm) of the water surface below the craft. As the craft moved slowly forward this depression of the surface moved with the craft, displacing water and creating waves. As speed built up the action of wave creation became more complex, but the key point is that waves were created and the craft's propulsion system had to produce a thrust to work against the wave-making drag on the hull, even though the bottom of the craft was not in contact with the water. The magnitude of the drag due to wave-making depends on the plan-form shape of the craft, the cushion pressure and the craft speed, and on water depth. It is sufficient to say here that 'wave drag' increases to a peak as speed increases and the then reduces steadily as speed increases further. This peak in the drag curve is known as the 'hump'. So, if you know the expression 'getting over the hump', that is the hump!

Thus, these various factors represent the basic theoretical ideas behind the amphibious hovercraft operating over water: powering the air cushion, providing thrust to overcome a combination of aerodynamic drag, momentum drag and wave drag, and of course to overcome additional effects caused by rough water. And all these factors vary with craft size, weight, shape and design features, suggesting at the outset that a lot of investigation was necessary in order to determine what a good, economic, Hovercraft design should look like. This was a little part of the challenge facing the hovercraft designers.

One question that was much discussed around this time was whether this vehicle that could cross land or water was a ship or a low flying aeroplane? When on water it could operate without touching the surface, even if it did create a lot of mist and spray. SR.N1 had been built using aircraft techniques, theoretical methods and materials. There was a good reason for this. The amount of power required to create the air cushion increases as a hovercraft gets heavier, so it is desirable to minimise the weight of the structure, engines, fans and so on. The low structure weight requirement pointed towards the use of high-strength aluminium alloys, and riveted construction since aircraft-type high-strength aluminium alloys are generally not weldable. In selecting Saunders-Roe to build the SR.N1, NRDC had chosen a company with a long history in the construction of flying boats. Post WW2 the company had built the SR.A/1 jet propelled fighter flying-boat and the huge SR.45 Princess flying-boat designed for non-stop transatlantic service by B.O.A.C., British Overseas Airways Corporation, quite apart from the SR.53 fighter propelled by a combination of turbojet and a rocket! The procedure in aircraft companies was that military aircraft were designed to meet the requirements for military aircraft, and civil aircraft to meet the requirements for civil aircraft. The British Civil Airworthiness Requirements (B.C.A.R.) were published by the Air Registration Board, the ARB. A Hovercraft equivalent was needed. According to Morris in his 1962 paper to The Institution of Engineers and Shipbuilders in Scotland, "A number of informal discussions had already taken place between senior officials of the Ministry of Transport, Ministry of Aviation, Hovercraft Development Ltd. and the firms constructing hovercraft in order that a certain degree of collaboration and approval of method of working could be assured from the Ministries concerned. A general consensus of opinion showed that the draft rules for designing, constructing and operating hovercraft should be based on the British Civil Airworthiness Requirements and accordingly the committees that had been formed set to work to draft rules which in due course were to be submitted to the A.R.B." Thus it came about that the design, construction and licensing of Hovercraft came under the oversight of the Air Registration Board, but in close co-operation with the Ministry of Transport, and especially with the Marine Division of that organisation.

In February 1962 the first sections of provisional British Civil Air-Cushion Vehicle Safety Requirements were issued. Even though a lot of experience could be brought to bear on the Hovercraft question much learning would be necessary by everyone involved, so discussions went on in committee with membership drawn from the Ministry of Transport, the Ministry of Aviation, Hovercraft Development Ltd., the Air Registration Board and with two representatives from the Hovercraft constructors.

Due to its work on SR.N1, Saunders-Roe based on the Isle of Wight was in the Hovercraft design and construction business from the outset. A licence was also issued by Hovercraft Development Limited to Vickers-Armstrong (Engineers) Ltd. based at South Marston airfield near Swindon, and a licence, for peripheral craft carrying up to a maximum of 20 passengers to a firm under the name of Samuel White. Ted Tattersall does not recall any hardware being produced by Samuel White. As a result this licence was transferred to Cushioncraft, a subsidiary of the aircraft manufacturer Britten Norman Ltd. based at Bembridge on the Isle of Wight. William Denny and Brothers Ltd. from Dumbarton became involved in 1960 and held the 'sidewall licence'.

As a final aside, observant readers may have noticed that in the illustration at the beginning of the chapter the designation painted on SR.N1 is SR-N1. Though much of the early 'paperwork' relating to Hovercraft used the designation with the 'dot', the designations painted on the various craft generally used a dash, as in SR-N1, and with even more variations in publications and advertising material.

Chapter 4

The Denny D.1 and D.2 Hovercraft

In October 1962, Charles F. Morris presented his paper 'SIDE-WALL HOVERCRAFT' to a meeting in Glasgow of *The Institution of Engineers and Shipbuilders in Scotland* (IESIS), and subsequently to the *Aberdeen Mechanical Society* in Aberdeen. The presentation started with a review of different methods of using the 'air cushion principle' and an explanation of Christopher Cockerell's ideas and how they might be applied, before going on to describe the involvement of William Denny and Brothers Ltd. with Hovercraft Development Ltd. and the application of the new air cushion vehicle technology in the design, construction and operation of the Denny D.1 and D.2 Hovercraft. The discussion that followed Morris's presentation was opened by E.G. Tattersall who, in the printed version of the paper, said the following: "Naval Architecture and the shipping industry have evolved over hundreds of years, of which certainly the last century has seen the greatest advances. Hovercraft, the newcomers to the field of transport, have only been in existence for a period of four years. One must, therefore, not judge them on present achievements, admirable though these may be considering such a short interval, but rather they should be judged on the potential for future craft". The reader should bear these words in mind when perusing what is told in this and subsequent chapters describing the efforts of the people in the Leven Shipyard at Dumbarton. William Denny and Brothers, with their subsidiary Denny Hovercraft Ltd., were given only three years. It is difficult and demanding to develop new concepts. It is only too easy to criticise, especially with the benefit of hindsight.

We cannot be certain of the exact sequence of events that brought the Denny Company into the Hovercraft business around the middle of 1960. In that year the company sold four ships, but only at a modest profit. In 1960, if not before, the Denny Board must have recognised that the company's outlook for trading conditions in shipbuilding and marine engineering was not good, and that new avenues for business needed to be sought. The Author's opinion on this must remain speculative, however, since it is very unlikely that Minutes of the Board Meetings survive. Probably the best explanation on how Denny became involved with Hovercraft was given by Ted Tattersall when he described how he was asked by Christopher Cockerell to champion the type of air cushion craft that contained the cushion between catamaran-like side keels or walls and only employed Cockerell's jet seals at the bow and stern. This type of craft had been the subject of some of Cockerell's early experiments and, while not amphibious, it could be propelled by marine propulsion devices and the power requirement to maintain the air cushion would be much less than for the corresponding amphibious version. Ted's investigations into the likely performance of such a craft encouraged HDL and NRDC to contact the highly respected Denny's of Dumbarton, who at that time were famous for their ferry boat and river boat designs.

There seems to have been sufficient confidence, probably from what was known already from experimental work by HDL and full-scale tests on SR.N1, that the air cushion sidewall craft would work well since there was an announcement in the July 28, 1960, edition of the *The Glasgow Herald* **'Dumbarton Firm to Build Hovercraft'** which went on to quote Denny Director Sydney Dale saying that the craft "would be rectangular in shape, with two long sides in the form of walls partially immersed in the water, and the cushion of air under the craft would be retained by these side-walls and a curtain of air at front and back". An artist's impression of what was intended showed a passenger-carrying sidewall Hovercraft of rectangular planform and significant size. This was the type of craft that eventually emerged, but before that, according to Ted, serious design work was carried out on a craft for a riverboat operator in India.

Morris's paper speaks lucidly of the uncertainties faced by the designers confronted with many aspects of Hovercraft design. One major uncertainty at the outset was the question of craft resistance due to wave making. In his paper Morris describes the work carried out in the Denny Test Tank, usually known at Denny's as the Experiment Tank, to define the best shape and configuration of the sidewalls of projected sidewall hovercraft. A model sidewall Hovercraft complete with air cushion was almost ready for testing when it was abandoned, probably temporarily, since in his Annual Report for 1960, Denny Experiment Tank Superintendent Hans Volpich viewed the model tests as part of a long term programme to investigate such questions as shallow water effects, stability, etc., so that extrapolation could then be made to larger commercial craft. To make more rapid progress the decision was taken to build a 60 foot long trials craft for outside testing, and to give more conclusive results for factors such as to the power required and craft stability. This craft became the Denny D.1.

D.1 Research Sidewall Hovercraft

The basic principle behind D.1 was that an air cushion would be trapped between the two sidewalls and by Cockerell's air jets at bow and stern.

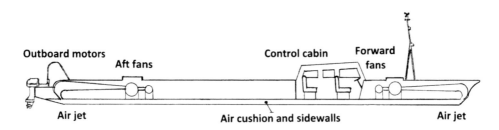

Schematic section through the Denny D.1 Sidewall Hovercraft

To minimise the power requirement for these jets it was logical to make their length as short as possible and therefore running straight across the craft at right angles to the sidewalls. The result was an air cushion with a rectangular planform. An illustration of the difference in the wetted area of D.1's hull, off and on the air cushion, is shown below.

Design work on D.1 started in June 1960 at the shipyard and with the air jet arrangements being handled by Hovercraft Development Ltd. Construction began in November and the craft was lowered onto the water at the Leven Shipyard in May 1961.

D.1 on Launch Day

The Glasgow Herald reported on May 27 that the Hovercraft had passed its open water test and had cruised at 16 knots during trials on the Gareloch.

The craft measured 63 feet in length and had a beam of 10 feet. The air cushion was 56 feet 4 inches long, giving a length to breadth ratio for the cushion plus sidewalls of 5.6, so D.1 was quite narrow compared with later Hovercraft. Though the craft needed to be light by shipbuilding standards, there was no reason to make particular efforts to reduce or optimise weight so the quickest, cheapest and most simple construction methods were chosen. The hull was made of marine gaboon plywood and mahogany and the air ducts and nozzles of sheet steel. The four fans were driven by two 25 b.h.p. water cooled engines and propulsion was by two Mercury outboard motors, initially of 35 b.h.p. each but later changed to larger units of 50 b.h.p. The cockpit, or control cabin, was designed to cater for three people - the driver and two test observers. Instruments were fitted to measure fan speeds, propeller speeds and thrust, cushion pressure at three points, the wave profile under the craft at 20 points along the craft, and trim and speed. Fitted out in this way and with crew on board, D.1 weighed a little over 4 tons, giving a cushion pressure of 16.9 pounds per square foot. Part of the hull was painted orange, but with blue and white stripes along the sides, divided by vertical black lines 5 feet apart. The purpose of these stripes and lines was to enable wave behaviour to be observed when the craft was moving.

D.1 worked well, in fact very well. In the good conditions required to get base-line measurements a speed of 17.6 knots was measured over the Gareloch measured mile, and almost 20 knots with the larger Mercurys fitted. Newspaper reports later claimed that a speed of 23 knots had been reached.

D.1 on trial in the Gareloch

In his 1961 Experiment Tank Report, Hans Volpich stated that "the decision to build a 60' fully operative model proved correct. The Press publicity alone given to the appearance of the Denny Sidewall Hovercraft Model D1 in the summer of 1961 was quite an asset for any future commercial plans. At the same time far more valuable data could be recovered in this manner than by any tests on small models. Unfortunately the publicity proved a certain drawback to the actual trials programme not to speak of the prevailing bad weather conditions in the summer of this year. The craft had to be used only too often for demonstration purposes to interested parties, which pushed the scientific trial programme somewhat into the background".

Another comment of interest in Volpich's report is that "Commercial testing and model tests for urgent shipyard proposals had to take priority in the tank programme and therefore the basic hovercraft model tests to a small scale had to be further delayed to the annoyance of Hovercraft Development Ltd." It was intended to devote time to this basic research early in 1962.

So, as stated by Morris in his IESIS paper, testing on the Clyde was adversely affected by poor weather in the latter part of 1961 and it was decided that the craft should be taken to the Hovercraft Development Ltd. base at Hythe on Southampton Water, with trials staffed by the technical group of HDL. This took some of the workload off the small number of Denny Tank staff available for the D.1 tests, notably the craft driver Geoff Wilkinson.

Photograph of D.1 prepared for transportation to Hythe in March 1962

It is also possible that the William Denny Brothers management considered that they had learned enough and really wanted to get on with the design and potential sales of the projected D.2 craft.

On 13th October 1961, a company memo from the Denny Board, circulated to all directors and managers in the company, stated that Denny Hovercraft Ltd. had been formally registered in Edinburgh, with the following Directors:

W.D.K. Marshall (Chairman of Denny's and also Chairman of the new enterprise)
F.R. Topping
S.D. Dale
C.F.Morris (Executive Director)
and Mr. H.F. Chatton as Secretary

"As soon as premises are near completion it is hoped to recruit a small labour force. Mr. H.P. Orr will be transferred from the Experiment Tank and will be responsible to Mr. C.F. Morris for the day-to-day running of the new company". This statement is from the original company memo, a copy of which is still held by Hugh Orr.

In 1963, Denny Hovercraft Chief Draughtsman Peter Macdonald made the comment to the Author that he thought that the William Denny Brothers Board had been lulled by the success of D.1 into the belief that the D.2 craft would be just as immediately successful, and delivered to the customer after a few weeks testing, as was normal shipbuilding practice. In an article in *The Glasgow Herald* on February 19, 1962, entitled **'Denny's Progress on Hovercraft - Second Model Ready for Summer'** (this referred to the D.2 craft), Morris was much more cautious, making no claims about the D.2 craft and only saying about D.1 that she "did more than was expected of her". The author of the article thought that this was quite an understatement! It was also stated in the article that Mr. Morris "is now training a team of Hovercraft builders". A factor that must have been bearing heavily on the William Denny Board was the rapidly deteriorating financial position of the company. D.2 craft had to be built and sold as soon as possible, so plans were in motion to build, in quick succession, four craft of the D.2 type. The results of this financial pressure are described later.

The D.2 series craft were designed at the outset as 'Hoverbuses', with a carrying capacity of about 70 passengers. The picture of the two models below gives an idea of the comparative sizes and appearances of D.1 and the proposed D.2. The D.2 model was one of an identical pair made for wind tunnel testing.

Display model of D.1 beside a wind-tunnel model of D.2

The D.2 craft were to be made of glass-reinforced plastic (GRP), and powered by marine diesel engines. In his 1962 IESIS paper Morris gave the overall length of the craft as 83 feet 6 inches, the overall width as 19 feet 3 inches and claimed an estimated service speed of 20 knots with full load. He said that prior to the material of construction being decided, experiments on GRP had been conducted over a period of six months. Following the successful conclusion of these experiments a large, well insulated and heated building shed was fitted out to enable construction to start. The plywood and GRP moulds for 'laying up' parts of the hulls can be seen in the photograph taken inside the shed, usually referred to incorrectly as the 'Fibreglass Shed' (Fibreglass was a trade name).

D.2-002 under construction in the 'Fibreglass Shed'

The internal construction of the sidewalls

These photographs are due to Denny Hovercraft manager Hugh Orr. They show the second of the D.2 series craft, D.2-002, and the much better working conditions than were typical of most shipyards (though it has to be said that glass fibre is not the most pleasant stuff to work with).

The layout of the D.2 craft as presented by Morris in his Glasgow lecture on Sidewall Hovercraft is shown below. In traditional ship design fashion it had engine rooms - machinery spaces - fore and aft. In his lecture, Morris pointed out the very adverse conditions in which all items of machinery had to operate. The fans drew air laden with salt spray into the fan rooms in the machinery spaces, which meant that all items on the craft had to be fully marinised. This pointed towards using diesel engines, the lightest marine diesels of the required power that could be obtained at the time, manufactured by the American company Caterpillar. The fans were driven by Caterpillar D.330 diesels and the German Schottel rudder propeller units on the craft's transom by the more powerful D.333 diesels. Where gear boxes were required they were also of an American type. The fans themselves were standard commercial items of the centrifugal type.

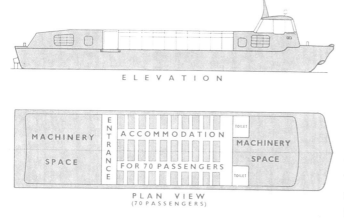

ELEVATION

PLAN VIEW
(70 PASSENGERS)

The passenger and crew entrance, with its lifting wing doors to port and starboard, and the passenger accommodation were located between the two machinery spaces. The bridge was set above the forward machinery spaces, affording an excellent all-round view. The craft was fully controlled from the bridge, which was accessed from the passenger accommodation by a door into the forward engine room and then by a short vertical ladder. Either one or two toilets, or a toilet and a pantry, were provided at the forward end of the passenger accommodation.

The main hull structure of the D.2 craft was, in essence, like an open flat bottomed barge with superstructure either end and a central passenger area covered by a canopy comprised of a welded aluminium frame with Perspex glazing, clear at the sides and orange overhead. The sidewalls were narrow catamaran-like extensions below the craft sides, which then combined with the bow and stern transverse air jet nozzles that created and maintained the air cushion below the hull.

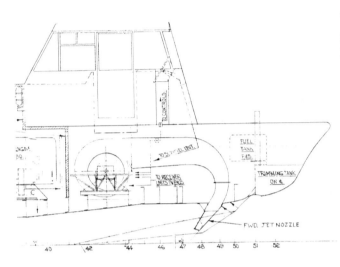

The arrangement of the bow nozzle is shown in the drawing, with the hull frame numbers for reference. This nozzle, at about frame 48, was extended below the hull by use of conveyor belting-like material, giving a degree of flexibility under wave impact. The air duct from the fan narrowed progressively from the fan to the nozzle outlet, which measured 2.75 inches in width.

One item that was the subject of much experimentation was what was known as the skeg, the removable and replaceable part of the sidewall at the forward end. Designed like this in case of the need for damage repair, the shape of the skegs was later cut back in order to try to divert spray around the craft sides.

Generally the sidewalls extended 22 inches below the flat bottom of the craft but this was increased to about 30 inches near the bow when the full depth skeg was fitted.

The aft nozzle, 5 feet 6 inches forward of the transom, was moulded into the GRP bottom at the rear of the craft with a 'turn down' to deflect waves from entering the nozzle. The Schottel rudder propeller units were mounted on the transom and driven by shafts from the two D333 Caterpillar diesel engines. The Schottel units, referred to for convenience in later chapters as 'zed drive units'

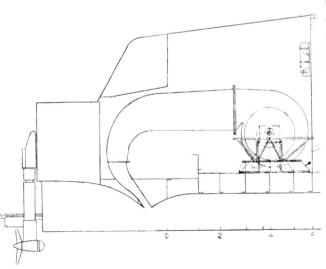

(even when not in the 'zed' configuration), allowed the little pods carrying the propellers to be rotated through 360 degrees in the horizontal plane, giving the craft a very effective manoeuvring capability. Initially, for normal 'ahead' operation the units were set so that propellers were 'pushers'. Later the pods were rotated through 180 degrees so that the propellers were in the 'puller' or tractor mode during normal 'ahead' operation. This had the advantage that the propellers were now operating in more or less clear water and still far enough behind the disturbance of the aft nozzle. The disadvantage was that the propellers were now without any protection from debris in the water.

This photograph shows the aft machinery spaces, one containing the two propulsion engines and the central engine for driving the group of fans in the aft 'fan room'. Immediately forward of the 'engine room' is the vestibule, giving access to the craft from outside and to the passenger accommodation.

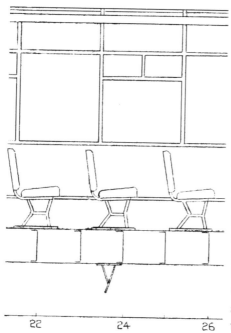

Though most of the D.2 craft structure was to be in glass reinforced plastic (GRP), large areas of the craft bottom and the internal decking were to be of marine plywood, fixed to moulded GRP channel section transverse beams that also connected the sidewalls together. Generally these channels were positioned 18 inches apart, resulting in a high degree of hull sub-division - a good feature in case of serious damage and resultant flooding. Another feature of the underside of the craft was a sort of transverse flap at a position midway between the forward and aft nozzles, made of a similar material to the extension of the forward nozzle and having a small degree of flexibility. Morris did not mention this in his IESIS paper but he did mention, in his section on Seaworthiness, that air cushion vehicles can have a condition of instability that can be corrected by splitting the air cushion into sections, in the case of the D.2s by this flap.

Due to the time being taken to build the first D.2 to the designed GRP standard, the decision was taken by the Denny Brothers Board to push the project forward by building the barge-like hull of the first craft, D.2-001, in wood. The results of this decision will be discussed in Chapter 5.

The D.2 series craft were much larger and heavier than the experimental D.1. With an air cushion length of 66 feet 3 inches from nozzle to nozzle and breadth between sidewalls of 17 feet 3inches, the all-up weight of 29.35 tons resulted in an air cushion pressure of about 52.4 pounds per square foot, again higher than D.1's value of 16.9 pounds per square foot. Taking the effective cushion width at waterline level as the combined width of the cushion and sidewalls gives an effective cushion length to breath ratio of 3.5. These factors meant that the performance and operating characteristics of the D.2 craft were significantly different from D.1 in a number of ways. To give an example, the higher cushion pressure meant that the D.2 craft created a lot more fine spray than D.1.

D.2-001 under test on the river Clyde off Dumbarton

The first of the D.2 craft, D.2-001, started its trials in July 1962, trials that did not start well when the craft was damaged while being lowered onto the water, and then took longer than expected due to the tests showing that modifications were necessary "to its hovering performance", and to its propulsion system, before final trials could begin. The trials with D.2-001 resumed in January 1963 but, following a towing test involving the Royal Navy, were abandoned in February. D.2-002 with its mainly GRP hull became ready for testing in April 1963.

D.2-002 on the Gareloch in 1963

Neither of the first D.2 craft carried more than the basic instrumentation that comprised the standard commercial items, primarily engine instrumentation, so speed testing over the Gareloch measured mile was limited to timing the craft over the measured mile with the propulsion engines running at set numbers of revolutions per minute (rpm). With 'pusher' propellers, the propulsion engines running at 1800 rpm and the craft at an all-up weight of 27 tons, D.2-001 achieved 18 kts. With 'puller' propellers, the same engine speed and at the same weight, D.2-002 achieved 21.5 knots. Increasing the craft weight to 30 tons reduced D.2-002's speed to 20.5 knots.

Hans Volpich's Annual Report for the Denny Experiment tank in 1962 included the statement that "As some trouble had been experienced with the pusher type Schottel units on D2 and as the masking effect of the vertical part of the unit on the propeller is unknown it was decided to make a thorough exploration of this". The report went on to say how this would be done, involving casting a propeller at Dumbarton, for use by Messrs. John Brown Ltd. of Clydebank in casting a bronze replica, and with the co-operation of the people from the Haslar Cavitation Tunnel. "The propeller will be tested under appropriate conditions with and without the Schottel unit to assess thrust, torque and efficiency in both conditions."

D.2 Data   (As quoted by Morris and in the September 1963 issue of *Air Cushion Vehicles*)

Craft overall length	83 feet 6 inches
Overall width of hull	19 feet 3 inches
Length of air cushion (Author's value)	66 feet 3 inches
(N.B. Variously quoted elsewhere as 66 feet 10 inches and 65 feet)	
Breadth of air cushion between sidewalls	17 feet 3 inches
Depth of sidewalls below the flat bottom	22 inches
Estimated weight with fuel and crew but without passengers	23.85 tons
Maximum deadweight	5.5 tons
Estimated service speed	25 knots
Total average service brake horse power	740 b.h.p.
Maximum draught to the bottom of the propellers when "off the cushion"	4 feet 6 inches
Maximum operating range	125 miles
Fuel tank capacity	200 Imperial gallons

D.2-002 leaving the Leven on trials, May 1963

So looking back after all these years and with the benefit of that wonderful thing, hindsight, what might be the initial assessment of the D.2 design?

Putting D.2-001 to one side, the D.2 design was in many ways a good workmanlike job by people who knew the sea and ships, not 100% right but a very good first attempt at designing and building something that had never existed before, a fully-commercial sidewall Hovercraft. However, it is often the case in engineering that the items that are not right, sometimes very few and in unexpected quarters, are the ones that come back to haunt the designers and builders. In the case of the D.2 design it would not have been expected that it was the reliability of the propulsion system that caused the most serious problems and bad publicity. But that is what happened.

Chapter 5

DHL

On Thursday 2nd May 1963 the Author joined the staff of Denny Hovercraft Ltd. and found himself among as pleasant a group of people as anyone could ever wish to work with. The Hovercraft design team was housed in a small group of wooden huts near one of the shipyard docks, with a slipway, crane

and a large black shed, the 'Fibreglass Shed' where the glass fibre laminating work was done and where D.2-004 was building. One of the D.2 series craft, D.2-003, was on blocks near the office, in the final stages of completion.

The Denny yard with the black Fibreglass Shed and the huts with D.2-003 just showing above them in the middle distance can be seen on the front cover in the photograph taken from the top of the ancient fortress of Dumbarton Rock.

Naval architect Hugh Orr, who had worked previously under the Experiment Tank Superintendent Hans Volpich, was the Denny Hovercraft Manager, also handling what could be described loosely as craft performance and naval architectural design matters. Peter Macdonald was the Chief Draughtsman, which belied his technical function of dealing with craft strength, and Dick Hartley was the Manager of the Fibreglass Shed. Peter was ex-aircraft industry with a stressing background, which was not inappropriate since certification of Denny and all other Hovercraft was under control of the ARB, the Air Registration Board. Dick Hartley was a genial Northumbrian from Newcastle. In over-all charge was Naval Architect and Denny Technical Director Charles F. Morris. Charles Morris had joined William Denny and Brothers in June 1960. He had been naval architect to the Orient Steam Navigation Company and had played a major part in the design of the 40,000 ton passenger liner *Oriana*, still building in 1960 at the Barrow-in-Furness yard of Vickers Armstrongs (Shipbuilders) Ltd. Though appointed naval architect at Dumbarton he remained responsible for the *Oriana* until her maiden voyage in December 1960. *Oriana* was constructed with over 1000 tons of aluminium in her superstructure, so Charles Morris brought this experience to Denny's.

It was in July 1960 that William Denny Brothers announced, after negotiations that started in May 1960, that the company would start a programme of research and development in collaboration with Hovercraft Development Ltd. The early work, on the experimental Hovercraft D.1 for example, was carried out in the shipyard offices until Charles Morris, or CFM as he was commonly known, built up and trained the small staff, mainly young, that became the core of Denny Hovercraft Ltd. - DHL.

The total office staff of DHL numbered about 17. Apart from the two secretaries, Manager Hugh Orr, and Dick Hartley in his Fibreglass Shed, the thirteen design and technical staff were housed in a pleasant office in one of the huts, with windows overlooking the River Leven and with a view of Dumbarton Rock. A short stretch of the River Clyde was visible between the Rock and McAllister's boat yard on the other side of the Leven. Everyone felt a degree of satisfaction in being connected with the Denny tradition, so that when the Clyde passenger steamer *Queen Mary II* appeared from behind Dumbarton Rock, on its summer schedule of daily cruises down-river to the open Firth, there would be a cry of "Denny boat", and everyone would look up to see the popular turbine steamer that had been delivered from the Denny yard in 1933.

Helen Auchterlonie was the senior of the two secretaries (for some reason the Author never discovered, Helen had been given the affectionate nickname 'Teuchtie'). Andy, the oldest member of staff, loved to reminisce about his days in charge of a Nile steamer. Hilary Watson and Malcolm McGregor were both keen yachtsmen and acted as the Hovercraft trials crew, and wrote trial reports when required. The others, all with a range of backgrounds and qualifications in ship building or naval architecture or mechanical engineering, or else working towards qualifications, carried out a variety of design tasks on the D.2 and the proposed D.3 craft. Andy and Peter Macdonald apart, we were all young, about thirty give or take a bit, and probably idealistic. Transport vehicles like ships or aircraft become almost like living things and people who labour in creating them often derive great satisfaction from their personal involvement, in whatever capacity.

The stressing work, that is to say the structural strength calculations, on the glass reinforced plastic D.2 had been done mainly by an engineer named Ronnie Ballantyne. He had left the company and the Author was his replacement as the 'Stress Engineer' on the DHL payroll, with a first task of roughing out the structure for the proposed D.3 craft. By 1963 standards D.3 was a big craft, 150 feet long, 50 feet in breadth, of welded aluminium construction, weighing 130 tons fully loaded with 525 passengers or 40 tons of freight, and with a maximum design speed of 40 knots in 2½ feet high waves.

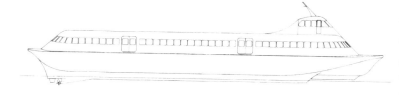

The drawing on the left is by the Author, based on the original general arrangement drawing with which he had to work.

The general appearance of the hull of D.3 can be judged from the drawing above and from the photograph of the large tank test model being investigated by Hovercraft Development Limited.

The evolution of the British Civil Air-Cushion Vehicle Safety Requirements has been described briefly in Chapter 3. In these Requirements the paragraphs dealing with structural strength had taken account of flying boat experience, since flying boats had light-weight structures and had to be designed to take off from and land on rough water, leading to high water impact pressures and loads on the hull. The Requirements contained two sets of equations which encapsulated what was known about this subject and gave the designers a basis for ensuring adequate structural strength. As might be expected, the input data to the equations were factors like craft speed, craft weight, and wave height and wave length, these last two giving a measure of wave size and steepness. The point at which the impact was assumed to occur had also to be specified, a bow impact being more severe than one occurring further aft.

One of the jobs in the office was 'Weights'. Track had to be kept of the weight of everything on the D.2 craft, so that the 'All Up Weight' and centre of gravity (C.G.) position of each craft were known and controlled. When sea trials were being conducted, for example, knowledge of these factors was essential. Even though not at the same stage of development, the same applied to D.3 and Dougie McNaught and Stewart McAllister in particular were involved in collecting together what could be said about the weights and weight distributions for D.3 - for items such as engines, propulsion components, fans, fuel, other equipment weights and of course payload. So, the Author was presented with what was known, or could be guessed, about the D.3 weight distribution.

In due course, using the Air-Cushion Vehicle Requirements, the various hull impact pressures, impact loads, hull shears and bending moments were calculated and a rough idea of the structure along the lines of the old type of egg-box drawn up. Two types of marine quality aluminium alloys known as NS4 and NS6 were being considered for manufacture of the structure. NS6 had the higher strength, but the problem was that it lost strength on welding. Another problem was that D.3 as originally conceived had a flat bottom, and flat plates are very poor at resisting pressure loads. What was needed was some form of arch shape, but there was insufficient clearance above the water for a single arch. What about having multiple arches, or might these trap the wave impact and concentrate the impact pressure even more? And what about draining any water that might enter the hull?

These issues are mentioned to give an indication of the potential size and scale of the work that lay ahead. In fact, we were at the beginning of what would have become a major development programme for Denny in the manufacture of light-weight welded aluminium hulls, and it took years for confidence to develop in this form of construction. However, this initial design work on D.3 led to a weight estimate for the bare structure, which was given to Peter Macdonald to be taken to one of the joint meetings arranged by HDL with the Hovercraft companies. When Peter came back from his trip south he said that our estimate of hull structure weight was very similar to one Vickers had quoted for their big VA-4 craft. Since VA-4 was to be an amphibious craft, admittedly with a somewhat higher speed than D.3, designed for construction using aircraft standard high strength alloys, this should not have been the case. The reason for this turned out to be that the Vickers Hovercraft Division practice was to design to higher structural impact loads than those specified by the Requirements to which we had worked. Such were the states of developments in these early days.

It is always good, if it can be arranged, to experience a vehicle in operation. So the Author made a request to go on one of the trials of the second of the D.2 series craft, D.2-002, which was being prepared for a voyage to London via the Caledonian Canal and the East Coast. This was approved and on a beautiful Sunday morning the Author joined Hilary, Malcolm and Captain Richard Mason beside D.2-002, which was in a wooden cradle beside one of the shipyard docks. A crane lifted the

cradle and lowered it and the craft into the water, allowing the D.2 to be eased out under the watchful eye of the little Denny tug called *The Second Snark*. We were soon on board and heading out through the mouth of the Leven, into the main channel past Greenock. Once past the Narrows at Rhu a succession of timed runs were made over the Gareloch measured mile, with only a stop for lunch. The sea conditions on the more open part of the trip between Greenock and the mouth of the Gareloch were a slight chop. Running over this was similar to being driven in a car at speed along a cobbled street. Conditions within the passenger cabin were pleasant, with some engine noise but otherwise like being in a green house with orange coloured glazing on the roof. In the Gareloch the water and the ride were smooth. Taken altogether, D.2-002 looked good.

Back in the office other aspects of the D.2s were spoken about. The primary concern was the life of the two zed drive units, mounted on the transom of each craft. These units were failing too frequently. The Author was told that the British Shipbuilding Research Association had been called in to assess the loads in the propulsion system and had found using strain gauges that there were torsional vibrations of an unacceptable level, and that if the engine speeds were kept at a certain value below what should have been the cruising setting these vibrations were at a minimum though not eliminated. This meant that D.2-002 could not run with the propulsion engines at full power and could not achieve its intended full speed of 25 knots. And even at reduced power the zed drive units kept failing. William Denny and Brothers Ltd. had an engine works in Dumbarton and the problem was discussed between personnel from DHL, the Engine Works and the manufacturer of the zed drive units. The Author has no direct knowledge of what was said at these meetings, but what was obvious was that there was a metal fatigue problem somewhere in the gearing system. Generally, metal fatigue is due to the applied loads and the corresponding stresses being too high, possibly made worse by poor surface finish and various metallurgical factors. One possible solution was to fit larger zed drive units, but with the drawback of more weight and more drag than from the existing units.

Another matter was the spray mist blowing round the front and sides of the craft as it sped along, partially obscuring the view from the windows even when running in calm water. There were two reasons for this. The first was that Cockerell's idea of the peripheral jet was bound to create spray around a craft operated on water. The second was that the bluff front of the D.2 design meant that much of the airflow and some of the spray tended to go up and over the craft rather than being diverted round the sides. The opinion in the office was that a Vee bow was needed, of the type on the D.3 tank test model. It must be recognised here that the D.2 design was only the second Hovercraft made by Denny's, based mainly on what had been learned from the experimental D.1. Looking back on what happened, it would have been much better if a proper prototype of a D.2 size craft in GRP had been built, thoroughly tested and modified in the light of experience, before going into full scale production of the developed commercial version. However, the financial state of William Denny and Brothers mitigated against this. Westlands reached their fourth design by way of single examples of the elegant SR.N2 and the very practical and effective military SR.N3 before a fully commercial design emerged, and though Vickers had run a service between Rhyl and Wallasey with their VA-3 in the summer of 1962, VA-3 was far from being a commercial proposition. So it should not be surprising that there were lessons to be learned, possibly even 'skeletons in the cupboard', and that other issues would come to light during the voyage to London. It was inevitable that developing this new technology would involve trials and tribulations.

The big 'skeleton' was D.2-001. The story told to the Author was that the construction of the glass fibre reinforced plastic D.2 was taking longer than expected (the Denny Board had wanted the craft to go into service in 1962), so the Board made the decision to construct the hull of D.2-001 using wood, though with a GRP superstructure, in an attempt to get the craft into service sooner. The financial position of the company will be described later, and it is very likely that this bad and ultimately costly decision was made primarily due to financial pressure. In a letter from C.F. Morris dated October 7, 1965, written in response to a somewhat inaccurate and critical article entitled 'Hovercraft - trials and triumphs' published in *The Scotsman* on September 28, 1965, the impression is that CFM had not been at all happy with the Board's decision. What made the matter worse was that the hull of D.2-001 was to be designed and built by the shipyard, taking it out of the hands of Denny Hovercraft Ltd. These were early days in developing Hovercraft technology and methods for calculating craft resistance, or drag, were still evolving. So any test that measured the force required to propel the craft over the water was potentially valuable. To make such full-scale resistance measurements Denny engaged the assistance of the Joint Services Hovercraft Unit and the Royal Navy fast patrol boat *Brave Borderer* under the command of Lt.Cdr. John Hardwick (*Air-Cushion Vehicles*, March 1963). *Brave Borderer* towed D.2-001 on a long line over the Skelmorlie measured mile and then on the quieter and more sheltered waters of Loch Long, and began a high speed run. One test point on the graph was obtained - a resistance value of 3370 pounds (including the drag of the zed-drive units) at 21.5 knots. Denny Hovercraft manager Hugh Orr was on board the craft during the tests and, in a letter to the Author, described what happened after that: "On reaching a certain speed *Brave Borderer* created a transverse wave with a very deep hollow into which D.2-001 fell, causing heavy slams. Tests were stopped and, by opening a small inspection hatch on the saloon deck, water was seen and it was discovered that the cellular bottom had been breached". The official story issued later was that the craft had hit a log in the water. While this may have been true, the Author is inclined to think that the real problem was that the wooden hull was grossly under strength.

The neglected hulk of D.2-001, with paint peeling, sat on the dock-side for many months. The craft can be seen on the front cover, in the picture of the yard taken from the top of Dumbarton Rock. A closer inspection by the Author yielded the following two pictures. Clearly, the transom had been torn off and a look underneath showed that the bottom had been damaged as well, as described by Hugh Orr; also that the internal transverse beams supporting the plywood bottom were 36 inches apart, not the 18 inches on D.2-002. This doubling of the width of unsupported plywood meant that, for the same water impact pressure, D.2-001's bottom had one quarter of the strength of D.2-002's. A veil was drawn over D.2-001.

D.2-001 had been a distraction from the work in the Denny Hovercraft office, even if the hull design and construction had been carried out by the yard. Not much was said about it. It was the sort of situation when people are unhappy about something, cannot find words to express their feelings, and just let out a low sigh. D.2-002 and her later sisters were much more workmanlike propositions, even allowing for the problem with the propulsion system, and big events were only a few days away, when D.2-002 would be demonstrated to the press and would leave the yard for the voyage to the Thames and London.

As was said at the beginning of this chapter, the Author was among as pleasant a group of people as anyone could ever wish to work with. There were interesting technical discussions about questions such as the use of super-cavitating propellers, or would water jets be a better idea? And of course the vee bow was universally agreed as a necessary development of the D.2 craft. Occasionally at lunch time a group would go to the Co-op restaurant on Dumbarton High Street, where an excellent lunch could be had at a reasonable cost. Other social occasions were of the hill walking variety - a summer evening climb up Ben Lomond, or the Cobbler at Arrocher. And the Black Bull at Milngavie was recommended as a good place for a sociable evening meal that could include an excellent pêche flambée. It was all very stimulating and refreshing.

A new recruit, Bill Gracie, joined the DHL office on 17 June. Bill was a young graduate engineer with aircraft experience, strengthening our capacity for dealing with stress issues and fitting well into the spirit of the office.

The departure of D.2-002 for London on 30th May was a major event, or in office parlance "A great juncture"! A description of the voyage and operation on the Thames is given in the next chapter, with a following chapter describing the subsequent events in the office and one that affected the whole Company of William Denny and Brothers.

Chapter 6

The Voyage of D.2-002 to London

Thursday 30th May, 1963: D.2-002 was lying at the pontoon in the dock adjacent to the Hovercraft offices and the Fibreglass Shed, fully prepared for the voyage to London and with a little pram dinghy on the superstructure over the aft machinery space. The words 'Thames Launches Ltd - A Denny Hovercraft' were painted on the craft's sides.

A few days before, on Sunday 26th May, the craft had been demonstrated on Loch Long to some 40 journalists and a beaming Christopher Cockerell. In command of the D.2 was Captain Richard Mason from the 'Queensferry Passage' fleet of ferries operated by Denny across the Forth estuary just up-stream from the Forth railway bridge.

Typical of the Press headlines that followed were "Hoverbus Ready for Trip to the Thames - Successful Final Trial on Loch Long"; and the *Air-Cushion Vehicles* supplement to *Flight International* described D.2-002 as "A Sidewall Craft of Great Promise", while reminding readers that William Denny had built the *Marjory*, in 1815 London's first passenger steamboat.

The plan for the voyage south was that the craft would go from the Leven Shipyard to the open Firth of Clyde and the Kyles of Bute, round Ardlamont Point into Loch Fyne and enter the sea lock of the Crinan Canal at Ardrishaig. After passing through the canal the craft would proceed to Banavie, near Fort William, and go through the Caledonian Canal to enter the Inverness Firth, the Moray Firth and the North Sea. Various stops for fuel and other supplies would be required on the voyage down the exposed east coast of the U.K., before entering the Thames Estuary and going up-river to the Thames Launches boatyard at Eel Pie Island.

The photographs of Captain Mason on the bridge and of the delivery crew show the complement for the trip to Ardrishaig. Reading from left to right, Mr. W. Keith Marshall, Chairman of William Denny and Brothers, Captain Richard Mason, John Alban of Thames Launches, James Kean, Frank O'Hara, Malcolm McGregor and Hilary Watson.

D.2-002 was due to leave the yard shortly after stopping time. When stopping time arrived workers crowded the side of the dock to watch the departure (Hugh Orr photo). From the Hovercraft office, a group rushed outside, got into cars, drove to Dumbarton Rock and climbed it as fast as possible (Not an easy thing to do in a hurry as anyone who has climbed the Rock will know). At 5:45 p.m. the craft cast off and passed below, heading for the Firth of Clyde and the Crinan Canal. The Author does not recall who took this photograph of the D.2 leaving Dumbarton, so apologies for not attributing it. In

addition to these still photographs, the events were being filmed by the Author, as he had been doing for some days previously, completely unofficially, on Standard 8mm Kodachrome stock using an Eumig cine camera fitted with a three lens turret. Since no-one seemed to have concerns about photographs of DHL activities being taken, the most was made of opportunities to record as much as possible. More will be said about this film later. Suffice it to say at this point that the first part of it covering the voyage to Inverness can be viewed on-line on the National Library of Scotland /Scottish Screen Archive web site under the title 'Denny Hovercraft'. (See Appendix 2)

As soon as the D.2 was well past, Ian Tulloch and the Author rushed back down the Rock, got into the Author's old Ford Prefect (The 100E version), and set off for Ardrishaig via the Loch Lomond road to Tarbert, Arrochar, the Rest and be Thankful and Loch Fyne. At Ardrishaig the locals were out in strength, awaiting the arrival of the D.2. The D.2 part of the trip is told best by the following extract from the craft's Log.

Thursday 30th May 1963

1745 hrs.	Cast off from Dumbarton for Ardrishaig.	
1830 hrs	Cloch Lighthouse.	1 cable
1850 hrs	Toward Lighthouse.	1 cable
1920 hrs	Kyles of Bute Narrows.	
1950 hrs	Ardlamont Point.	
2055 hrs	Entered Crinan Canal sea lock and proceeded to No. 3 lock.	
2135 hrs	Finished with engines.	

There was a minor problem with a sea water inlet that delayed the craft by 15 minutes at one point.

Ian Tulloch and the Author watched the D.2 coming in and then squeezing through the locks at Ardrishaig, with Mr. Marshall on the bridge wing and Hilary and John Alban handling the ropes and fenders at the bow. After getting more film 'in the can' we had to leave for the journey back to Dumbarton. There was very little news until late next day, so again the story is best told by the D.2 Log.

Friday 31st May 1963

0630 hrs	Cast off; proceeded to No. 4 lock.
	(There were a few tight moments going through the canal before the craft was again in sea water)
1030 hrs	Departed from Sea Lock, Crinan. Set course for Dorus More 330° (Magnetic).
1045 hrs	Course 010° (Mag).
1115 hrs	Passed Easdale 5 cables.
1153 hrs	Railway Pier Oban.
1345 hrs	Cast off. Proceeded out of Oban Bay. Passed eastward of Maiden Island. Courses various to Appin Pier.
1420 hrs	Off Appin Pier. Set course round Shuna Islands to Corran Narrows.
1505 hrs	Through Corran Narrows.
1540 hrs	Entered Sea Lock Caledonian Canal
1620 hrs	Passed through double locks Corpach.
1845 hrs	Berthed in Canal above Neptune's Staircase.

In the office on the day following our trip to Ardrishaig there was no news until late afternoon when we heard that the craft was at Corpach. This time alone, the Author pointed his little Ford north by Loch Lomond, Crianlarich, Rannoch Moor and Kinlochleven to Fort William and the succession of locks known as 'Neptune's Staircase' at Corpach. The Hovercraft had been worked up the staircase

and was now tied up in the Caledonian Canal, beyond the top lock, with Ben Nevis looking magnificent in the back ground.

Once again, the photographer, probably Malcolm or Hilary, must be thanked for this picture. As at Dumbarton, the Author was still filming in 8mm cine. He had been asked to deliver a small package to the crew, so going on board it was learned that they were going to leave at 6:30 next morning, which presented a problem. To film the passage of the craft from beside the canal it was necessary to use the car to 'hedge hop' along the route, and it would have been a very understanding B&B establishment that would have allowed anyone to leave early enough to rendezvous with the D.2. But the weather was set fair, very fair indeed, so why not sleep out among the heather? The first 'shooting spot' was selected a little further along the canal, not far from a dry mound with heather on top, and the Author slept soundly in his sleeping bag until daybreak, with plenty of time to get organised before the rendezvous with the Hovercraft.

The weather on Saturday 1st June was perfect - clear air, blue skies and little or no wind. At about 6:45 a.m. D.2-002 appeared round a bend in the canal, against the back-drop of Ben Nevis with snow still filling the high corries. The routine for the day was: Take the film shots, pack up, run to the car and drive to the next possible vantage point - first another stretch of the canal, then Gairlochy with its lock gates still operated by manually driven capstans, followed by another superb viewpoint above Loch Lochy.

D.2 appears round a bend in the canal   *Waiting to enter the lock at Gairlochy*

D.2-002 Log, Saturday 1st June 1963

0630 hrs	Cast off.
0725 hrs	Gairlochy locks.
0755 hrs	Out of Gairlochy

The Caledonian Canal is mainly a succession of three lochs, first Loch Lochy in the west, then Loch Oich and finally Loch Ness, joined by man-made canal sections running in an almost perfect straight line along the geological fault that created the Great Glen. All vessels in the canal sections were subject to speed restrictions, but in the open water of Loch Lochy the D.2 could travel as fast as she was able.

The BP company had a policy of promoting Hovercraft, and as a part of this BP had commissioned a film company to record sections of the voyage of the D.2 to London. We met up on the same vantage point above Loch Lochy, where the camera crew told the Author how difficult it had been keeping up with the Hovercraft on the previous day. Apparently it had been "the first hovercraft that kept to time". A quick study of a map soon shows that the sea route was much more direct than going by the roads taken by the BP crew.

Below on Loch Lochy, D.2-002 duly appeared, looking great and travelling at impressive speed. Once again, it was get film 'in the can', pack up, run to the car and drive on, this time to the locks at Laggan, at the east end of Loch Lochy, just in time to film the craft coming in. At Laggan, the Author joined the craft and stayed on board through the beautiful tree-lined Laggan Avenue, then at low and high speed in Loch Oich, and along more canal sections to the succession of five locks at Fort Augustus. With the Ford Prefect still at Laggan this presented a transport problem, but not something to be concerned about on a day like this. The solution was the time-honoured procedure of hitching a lift back to Laggan, probably helped by the fact that the Author was carrying a camera on a tripod.

D.2-002 Log, Saturday 1st June 1963

0830 hrs	Laggan locks (2 locks)
0855 hrs	Laggan swing bridge
0930 hrs	Cullochy (2 locks)
1000 hrs	Kytra lock.
1015 hrs	Fort Augustus (5 locks)
1115 hrs	Left Fort Augustus (1125 - 1140 waiting for the BP film unit)

The passage of the D.2 down the five Fort Augustus locks, where the D.2 was very much a tourist attraction, gave adequate time to reach the next vantage points, first a Loch Ness beach and then a hillside above Castle Urquhart with a good view over a part of the loch that is over a mile wide. The shots from the beach went well, then nothing happened, or more correctly it was a long wait before the D.2 came into sight, creeping along the far side of Loch Ness as far as possible from the tourist traffic on the busy A82. Clearly, something was wrong.

D.2-002 Log, Saturday 1st June 1963

1205 hrs	Zed drive unit failure.
1510 hrs	Dochgarroch lock.

Once into the canal section at the north-east end of Loch Ness and past Dochgarroch lock there was little external sign of any problem with the D.2 and the craft proceeded to Muirton basin under the interested gaze of what appeared to be a substantial part of the population of Inverness! The Log entry was:

1630 hrs	Secured at head of Muirton locks to commence repairs.

During the evening Captain Mason demonstrated the craft lifting on its cushion and was totally relaxed about people of all ages clambering over the outside of the craft.

DHL at Dumbarton was advised about what had happened and a work party was organised to bring a new zed drive to replace the failed unit. Still taking pictures, the Author stayed on till Sunday morning before departing on the journey back to Dumbarton.

Following the D.2 down the East Coast was not possible. The essence of this part of the voyage can be gleaned from these remaining extracts from the Log of D.2-002 and from knowledge of the ports of call on the way south.

D.2-002 Log, Monday 3rd June 1963

1050 hrs	Engineers reported repairs completed.
	High seas prevented departure.
2300 hrs	Cast off from the entrance to the Sea Lock.

Tuesday 4th June 1963

0625 hrs	Arrived Fraserburgh No.3 dock.

Wednesday 5th June

	Fraserburgh High seas / or fog.

Thursday 6th June

0605 hrs	Left Fraserburgh for Aberdeen.
1000 hrs	Entered Aberdeen harbour.
1230 hrs	Left Aberdeen.
	Off St. Abbs Head 4-6 ft confused sea. Damage to craft.
	Electrical storm.
2400 hrs	Berwick. Berthed in Tweed Dock.

Friday 7th June

	Craft on slip for inspection.

Saturday 8th June

	Repairs to craft bottom.

Sunday 9th June

0430	Fog. Commenced un-slipping. Fog all day.

The planned ports of call after Berwick-on-Tweed were Whitby, Hull, Wells in Norfolk, Harwich, Isle of Grain (B.P. Kent refinery) and the Festival Pier on the Thames. According to the Thames Launches record the craft by-passed Wells and went direct to Great Yarmouth instead, before going on to Harwich, where the craft was delayed by a period of un-serviceability. (Zed drive unit again?) Mr. W.B. Caisley, Director of Thames Launches, joined the complement for the trip up river to London, where D.2-002 arrived on 15th June after a voyage of 829 miles, and made her way to the Thames Launches boatyard on the delightfully named Eel Pie Island at Twickenham. There the craft underwent some repairs and modifications, including painting the canopy top a matching pale blue to cut down heat transmission to the passenger cabin, and removal of the mast to allow passage under the Thames bridges at all states of the tide. Passenger carrying operations began on Monday 1st July. Five hundred passengers were carried that day, including the Lord Mayor of London, the pioneer airman Lord Brabazon of Tara and the writer and politician Sir Alan Herbert. Possibly more significant were the parties of port officials from New Orleans and senior police officers from the Thames Division, as reported in the July issue of *Air-Cushion Vehicles.*

Back at Dumbarton, spirits in the office were high, even though there had been a general lack of information on the progress of the D.2 down the East Coast and on the Thames. Talking to Peter McDonald about this, Peter observed that the management at Denny's did not see much need for passing on progress reports to the people in the Hovercraft team. This was annoying. The D.2 was their baby and not saying how she was getting on was not a positive contribution to morale. More was found out when Malcolm and Hilary returned, and when they wrote a report on observations from the trip and on lessons learned on the behaviour of D.2-002, sometimes in situations well beyond the conditions with which she was designed to cope. However, despite this minor irritation things at Denny Hovercraft Ltd. were going well.

A river tour with a difference

SEE LONDON BY HOVERCRAFT

ON THE DENNY D2 HOVERBUS

FROM THE FESTIVAL PIER TO TOWER BRIDGE

THE DENNY D2
operated by
THAMES LAUNCHES LTD
on
BP FUELS & OILS
LONDON'S FIRST COMMERCIAL HOVERCRAFT SERVICE

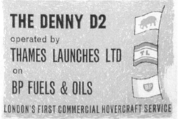

As noted above, after arriving at the Thames Launches yard in mid-June, about two weeks were spent preparing, and where necessary repairing, the craft for operation on the river. These operations with fare-paying public on board began after the VIP and press event on 1st July and continued through September, though with interruptions. On 15th September, while on a short holiday, the Author was back on board D.2-002 and given the run of the vessel by John Alban, who was the Driver that day, while the craft ran trips along the river. The crew included a cabin attendant in airline style uniform. The 8mm camera was

back in use filming the experience of the D.2 Thames operation.

Generally successful though the Thames operations were, and Mr. Caisley of Thames Launches was very enthusiastic about them, they were not without occasional and annoying problems. Anyone who remembers the Thames from that time will have been aware of the rubbish floating on the river, sometimes extending to

raft-like collections of wood from the docks. Damage to the propellers of small craft such as the Thames pleasure launches was frequent, even though these propellers were protected by the vessels' hulls and were sometimes mounted within tunnels. D.2-002's propellers mounted facing forward on the exposed zed drive units were very vulnerable and were subject to damage. This meant that the craft Driver had to keep a good look-out and steer clear, or cut the air cushion and use the resulting very good braking effect. While at speed on the air cushion the D.2 ran faster than the norm on the river while making less wash than displacement vessels. However, her speed was of concern to some river users and there would occasionally be a call of "Waterman, cut your speed".

There is much more to be told of what happened to D.2-002, and for that matter D.2-003, but that will have to wait for further chapters on the development of the four D.2 series craft. The next part of the story concerns the work in the Hovercraft Office and the Fibreglass Shed during the latter part of that eventful summer of 1963.

Chapter 7

The Thunderbolt and after

When Hilary and Malcolm came back from crewing D.2-002 on her way south they produced a report containing many observations on how the craft had performed and what defects, either in design or by failure, had occurred. In the section on craft handling the observations included the following on operation in heavy weather.

> The craft performs much better with the seas aft of the beam - these waves can be up to 8 feet high and can be coped with easily, ...

> Travelling into large waves isn't satisfactory. However, if it is necessary to sail the forward fan should be kept at 2000 r.p.m. - aft fan 1800 r.p.m. and propulsion engine r.p.m. to be kept fast enough to maintain very slow headway.

> In a following sea it is possible to surf for long distances on the backs of large waves by careful adjustment of propulsion engine r.p.m.

It is necessary to interject here that this was a craft designed for operation "in smooth water conditions to be found on rivers, lakes and in sheltered coastal waters"! This quotation is from C.F. Morris's letter written on October 7, 1965 to *The Scotsman*. Other observations could be described as the normal 'snagging' that occurs with any new vehicle, or even a house for that matter.

> A fixed fender at each bow and stern quarter is essential. Recently there has been an editorial in *The Daily Telegraph* deploring the fact that we travel with our fenders over the side.

> The lifting entrance doors are a curse - not only are they difficult to operate and keep watertight but frequently they can't be opened when the craft is alongside piers etc.

> The lifebuoys on the sides of the craft canopy are a great nuisance while working the craft - they should be put in a recess.

> During the demonstration to the Lord Mayor, there were 90 people on board. This was equivalent to an All Up Weight of 31.6 tons. The craft did lift but it was definitely overloaded.

Overall, considering the conditions to which it had been subjected, D.2-002 had done well, and the voyage should have been generally regarded as something of a triumph or at least a major achievement. It would have been a miracle if there had been no defects or adverse comments of any kind.

One item that was recorded in D.2-002's log was the damage to the craft's flat bottom, occurring in heavy weather between Aberdeen and Berwick and requiring the craft to be slipped at Berwick for repairs. This event diverted the Author from work on the big D.3 and led to increasing involvement with various aspects of the strength of the D.2 series craft and the certification process for D.2-003 in particular, while others in the office dealt with matters relating to D.2-002.

Calculations on the strength of the flat marine plywood bottom of D.2-002 indicated that, for its design conditions, it did not quite meet the Air Cushion Vehicle Safety Requirements. During repairs at Berwick, Malcolm and Hilary had had longitudinal battens, or stringers, glued and screwed to the lower surface of the marine ply bottom. In terms of strength, this was beneficial since it gave much better support of the ply panels, and they said it appeared to assist the craft when accelerating to get above hump speed, but at the cost of extra weight and possibly compromising water-tightness to some extent. This modification was to be applied to D.2-003, still on blocks beside the Hovercraft Office; and the craft was to be subjected to a proof bending test, as had D.2-002 before it. This test was to simulate the worst hull bending that was expected to occur in service.

The test procedure included the measurement of hull deflections relative to wires stretched at constant tension along the two sides of the craft. Loading the craft was by setting drums of resin from the Fibreglass Shed at defined positions in the cabin and then jacking the craft up at positions near the bow and stern. The test went well but there was some concern when analysis of the test results showed that, when unloaded again, the craft had not quite returned to its original 'straightness'. The little two ton capacity tensile testing machine and Hounsfield extensometer belonging to Denny Hovercraft and kept in Peter Macdonald's office were brought to bear on the question, by testing samples of glass reinforced plastic (GRP) similar in layup to D.2-003's sidewalls. It was found that when loaded to a stress similar to that under the conditions of the proof bending test the GRP samples did indeed stretch and continue to stretch, so that when unloaded they did not quite return to their original length. However, if the samples were left unloaded they did gradually return to their original length. It was all very interesting, and nothing to worry about, but things were about to change, and not for the better.

On Tuesday 23rd July, 1963, we were all called to a meeting in the shipyard offices. When we arrived outside the building people were flooding out from a previous meeting and it was obvious that something was seriously wrong. One man became faint and had to be helped. Gathered inside, we were addressed by a senior company official, the Author cannot remember which but probably it was Mr. W. K. Marshall, the company Chairman. The news he brought to us was devastating. The long-established and highly-respected shipbuilder William Denny and Brothers Ltd. had been placed in voluntary liquidation.

The reasons for this decision were explained, point by point. These were repeated in a letter to the stockholders, written by the Company Secretary H.F. Chatton and dated 12th August 1963.

"Following a Board Meeting held in Dumbarton on Tuesday, 23rd July, 1963, the following statement was issued to the Press:-

The Board of William Denny and Brothers Limited, having considered the present position of the Company and also the future prospects for Shipbuilding and Marine Engineering, have at a meeting today decided with the greatest reluctance that, in the absence of remunerative orders, there is no alternative open to them but to recommend that the Company should be put into Members' Voluntary Liquidation, and that a Meeting of the Stockholders should be convened for this purpose as soon as possible.

On the basis of the information presently available, the Board is advised that the Company's liabilities will, in due course, be met in full ... and will depend to some extent on the proceeds to be realised from sale of industrial land, buildings and plant, and from the Company's investment in its subsidiary, Denny Hovercraft Ltd."

The document went on to state that the subsidies offered by foreign countries to their own shipyards made it virtually impossible for British shipbuilders to obtain any share of these markets; also that new shipyards were being built in many countries as part of a policy of economic nationalism for political prestige. Apart from these factors bulk carriers were getting bigger, making an even larger proportion of them beyond the capacity of the Leven Shipyard; and there was a virtual closing of the market for shallow draft river craft, of which type it had built nearly 600 vessels prior to the Second World War.

"There was also a greatly reduced rate of ordering of Naval vessels for the Admiralty and of Cross Channel Vessels.

To operate economically the Company needed not less than three substantial ship orders each year, with an equivalent amount of Marine Engineering work. The numbers of ships delivered in recent years were:

1959	3 ships	Profit	£112,800
1960	4 ships	Profit	£71,800
1961	2 ships	Profit	£67,800
1962	1 ship	Loss	£245,200
1963	1 ship	-	-

After the delivery in 1963, which occurred in March, the only remaining vessel, with the exception of the steel hull of a small yacht, was a vessel building to your Company's own account, No.1504 ... Well over £1,000,000 had been spent on modernising the shipyard in recent years and the results in lower costs and improved efficiency have made themselves evident." The letter then went on to describe the extreme difficulties the firm had faced in obtaining new contracts, before describing the position of Denny Hovercraft Ltd., which will be now be given in full.

"Some three years ago, when your Board was endeavouring to find suitable projects to diversify your Company's activities, an agreement for a joint development programme was entered into with Hovercraft Development Limited, a wholly owned subsidiary of the National Research Development Corporation. Resulting from this an experimental craft 60 feet in length was completed in June 1961, and successfully demonstrated the Hovercraft principle. Your Board then felt justified in continuing work on Hovercraft with a new series of seventy passenger craft designated D.2. The first of these is now in operation on the Thames, having made, under its own power, the journey of over 800 miles from the Clyde. In spite of difficulties encountered, this Hovercraft has been seen by many people and considerable interest has been shown. Two other craft of the same type are at present in an advanced state of construction in Dumbarton. A considerable amount of design work has been carried out in conjunction with Hovercraft Development Ltd. on a substantially larger craft - D.3 - with a payload of about 40 tons. As with many new developments, progress tends to be slower than hoped and the point has not yet been reached, at which commercial orders have been obtained. Nevertheless your Board believes that the three craft of the D.2 type will find Buyers and that in due course there will prove to be a wide market for both D.2 and D.3 types. They earnestly hope that it will be possible for satisfactory arrangements to be made for design and development work to continue and that ultimately commercial production will be justified."

It was a very sober Denny Hovercraft team that returned to the office. Though the yard was going to close, the statement had a degree of optimism about the future of Denny Hovercraft Ltd. Having said this, the atmosphere in the office was sombre. It did not take much imagination to realise that without a major injection of capital the D.3 project was dead. Among the headlines in the papers over the following days were "DENNY'S GO INTO LIQUIDATION - Sale of Assets to Meet Shipyard Liabilities", "UNECONOMIC BUSINESS: HOVERCRAFT COSTS". It seemed for a time that there might be a development of the D.2 type, as indeed there was for a time with D.4 and D.5 study projects, craft with vee bows and other features that reflected the experience of D.2-002 on the North Sea and Thames, but it was not long before realisation dawned that work would be limited to selling off the three D.2 craft and, if possible, Denny Hovercraft Ltd itself. Clearly this would not be a good career path for any of us. For the younger members of the office, with no family or financial responsibilities this was not too serious, since jobs for qualified people were not in short supply. For older people with mortgages and family to support it was a much more serious situation.

For all of us it was a question of looking for another job. The picture shows some of the group in the office 'post liquidation'. (Reading from left to right: Ian Dunn, Ian Hall, Author, Peter Macdonald, Andy Morrison, Bill Gracie, Iain Tulloch, Malcolm MacGregor, Stewart McAllister and Dougie McNaught).

So, gradually people disappeared from the office. For those left there was still work to be done - such as carrying out a series of tests, greatly assisted by Dick Hartley, on samples of glass reinforced plastic (GRP) laminate to confirm and extend the knowledge of the strength and stiffness properties of the material used in the construction and certification of the hulls from D.2-002 onwards. The report on these aspects covered tensile, compression, flexure and shear behaviour of the GRP laminate. Very regrettably, due to the effect of the liquidation announcement, Dick Hartley suffered a minor heart attack.

One day a small group of men arrived in the office and became involved in discussions with Peter Macdonald. They represented a company that wished to run river cruises on the Nile, to the temples at Abu Simbel. This was regarded as a serious enquiry and we had to look into the question of transporting at least one D.2 from Dumbarton to the Nile by ship. We had only one cradle, made of wood, and of somewhat doubtful strength in the Author's opinion. The craft had no attachment points by which it could be lifted, so transport would require a cradle. But a good cradle would be expensive, and if more than one craft were to be exported there would be the cost of another cradle or the return transport of the original. But D.2-003 had already been lifted, more or less by its ends and with a substantial extra load amidships so why not add lifting points to the hull? To cut a long story short, this is what was done. Stainless steel fittings were fixed to the outside of the sidewalls, using fasteners called Huckbolts that could be set from outside since there was insufficient internal access to the sidewalls. To confirm the use of Huckbolts in this way required another series of tests to be put in hand. An interesting aspect of this work was that the fittings were at the interface between Hovercraft (aircraft) strength standards and the very different standards for ordinary commercial lifting gear.

In due course Charles Morris, Peter Macdonald, Andy Morrison, Bill Gracie and Ian Tulloch took up positions with Vickers at Barrow-in-Furness, Hugh Orr joined Vosper Thorneycroft as Test Tank Superintendent, and some people were offered jobs in other Clyde yards. This was still the period when the bustling river was lined with quays and yards of all descriptions. Before he left Dumbarton, Charles Morris took everyone for lunch at the Dumbuck Hotel on the outskirts of the town.

Alan Bingham, Chief Designer in the Vickers Hovercraft Division at South Marston in Wiltshire, came to interview all the technical staff for possible jobs in his organisation. As it turned out, the Author was the only one who accepted, a decision based on the belief, or was it simply an impression, that Vickers intended to develop sidewall hovercraft as well as the amphibious type. But more of that later.

In August there was a minor launching from the yard - minor in the sense that it was witnessed by little more than a dozen people. The vessel in question was a yacht hull, built by Denny's to the order of J. Silver's yard on the Gareloch. It was not a launch involving a lady smashing a bottle of champagne on the hull, followed by the ship gradually building up speed and entering the water. The yacht was standing on a single way, which looked very precarious, and was very reluctant to move. Eventually, it had to be pushed by a mobile crane to get it into the water. The finished yacht was to be called *Mary Fisher*.

The pictures above show the 'Mary Fisher' in the building shed and during launching.

Round about the same time, one of the shipyard workers took some of us to have a look at the hull of 1504, on which all work had ceased. Standing inside one of the holds of this 'great thing', this ship, it was difficult not to be overcome by the sad knowledge that the skills that had conceived, designed, planned and built this last of the Denny boats had been cast to the four winds. This included the staff of the first-class experimental establishment that was the Denny Experiment Tank.

Completion of Ship No. 1504 was taken over by the firm of Alexander Stephens, being launched from the Leven shipyard on 27th February, 1964, and completed as the 11,000 ton cargo vessel *Melbrook.*

In September 1963 the Author took a short and unpaid holiday and drove south, partly with the intention of taking cine film of D.2-002 on the Thames. As mentioned earlier he was welcomed

Hovercraft Development Ltd. premises at Hythe.

aboard by John Alban of Thames Launches and obtained a satisfying amount of 'footage'. Another reason for going south was to visit Hovercraft Development Ltd. at Hythe on Southampton Water. The HDL establishment turned out to be based in a collection of war-time buildings, comprising some Nissan huts and other buildings of the common brick-built construction that can still be seen at many sites round the U.K. At HDL, the Author was shown round by Ralph Hayward. The really exciting demonstration was of a model hovercraft with a 'fingered skirt'. This skirt was very flexible, behaved almost like a brush when running over obstacles and reduced the cushion air gap close to almost zero. With the great reduction in the air supply to the cushion offered by this invention, the potential benefits were obvious. The fingered skirt was a very important innovation. Apart from this the Author was given a short length of the flexible skirt made for the D.3 model. D.3 had been conceived with a short flexible skirt similar but of improved construction to that on D.2.

Back at Dumbarton there was a short lull in the necessary things to be done. The time was used to get John Orr, Hugh Orr's brother, to make a small water tank with a glass side and also a basic sidewall hovercraft model in the form of a box with a fingered skirt at one end and the sample of the D.3 model skirt at the other, and with a clear Perspex sidewall. The air supply to the cushion was from the Author's old Hoover 'Bomb' vacuum cleaner. Watching and comparing the behaviour of the fingered skirt and the D.3 'jetting skirt' was very illuminating. The fingered skirt behaved beautifully, and fingers were definitely the way ahead. A brief and illustrated explanation of the development of flexible skirts is given in a later chapter.

Another action on return from the south was to complete as much as possible of the 8mm cine film. This was given three showings to people who were still at the yard to wind things up, in one of the Experiment Tank offices, now part of The Scottish Maritime Museum.

There were very few of us left in the office by the end of 1963. The Author had arranged to join the Vickers Hovercraft Division on January 20th in the belief that the South Marston team was seriously interested in developing sidewall craft. This may seem like becoming an excessively personal bit of the story but there is a reason for telling it. Hilary Watson was inclined to stay with Denny Hovercraft to see what happened. At the very least, work needed to be done on D.2-002 and D.2-003 if they were to be sold. By this time it had been decided that the partly completed D.2-004 in the Fibreglass Shed would be retained but not finished, which was a pity because the support beams for the propulsion engines had been set at a different angle to allow the zed drive units to be mounted behind the sidewalls, greatly improving their protection from debris if nothing else. Even with Denny Hovercraft Ltd. being in such a sad state and with little or no career prospects for anyone remaining with the company, it was a great wrench leaving the Leven Shipyard and Dumbarton.

Chapter 8

1964 onwards

By the beginning of 1964 only a few of the Denny Hovercraft team remained in the office or the Fibreglass Shed, and there were very few signs that the business would be developed or even maintained, except as a 'going concern' for eventual sale. It was inevitable that everyone had given thought to their work and career prospects following the notice of liquidation of William Denny and Brothers. These thoughts had intensified as time went past and the outlook for a future with Denny Hovercraft Ltd. became progressively more uncertain as Charles Morris, Peter McDonald, Ian Tulloch, Bill Gracie and Andy Morrison moved to Vickers at Barrow-in-Furness and Hugh Orr left for Vosper. The next few paragraphs in the tale of what happened to DHL may appear excessively personal and detailed, but they are the lead-in to later events.

It was Hilary Watson who had coined the term 'Hover Fever', an affliction that was experienced or showed itself in different ways - in conversations in the office about aspects of Hovercraft design, or lying awake at night thinking about improvements that should or could be made to the D.2s, or what the appearance and details of future Hovercraft, in particular sidewall craft, might be. It was an affliction that was contagious and the Author had picked up the contagion, so that when Alan Bingham of Vickers came to the office in August to interview everybody and said that Vickers had an interest in sidewall craft, as well as in the amphibious types like their VA-2 and VA-3, the opportunity of joining the Vickers Armstrong Hovercraft team had to be taken seriously.

So, on 20th January 1964 the Author rejoined Vickers, this time Vickers Armstrongs (Engineers) Ltd. at South Marston airfield near Swindon in Wiltshire. There, the design office was just like the one he had left at Weybridge almost nine months before - very large and open-plan, without windows and with a raised line of offices at the back where the heads of departments worked, and presumably could overlook everyone. The design office structure was typically 'aircraft', with sections dealing with aerodynamics, stress, systems, design, weights and so on - each with its Chief. It was not surprising that it was like this since this was the organisation that in its earlier history had created the *Spitfire*, been bombed out of its works in Southampton and had gone on to develop jet aircraft like the Supermarine *Attacker, Swift* and *Scimitar*. The *Scimitar* was now nearing the end of its life with the Royal Navy, and from time to time one would come in for repair, overhaul or modification. Recognising that the organisation at South Marston would not design another aeroplane, it had diversified into new avenues like freeze drying, nuclear work, and of course Hovercraft.

It very quickly became obvious that there was little serious intention by Vickers to develop sidewall Hovercraft, and this realisation was made worse by the weather. For the Author's first January week at South Marston there was continual fog. The dark and the fog discouraged leaving his hotel in Highworth in the evening so the Author started sketching out thoughts on a follow-up to D.2, and writing letters, initially to Hilary at Dumbarton and to Ted Tattersall at Hovercraft Development Ltd. It was soon learned that Ted was trying to hold his 'sidewall group' together, and that he had "taken some of his lads out on D.2-002 from Portsmouth", only to experience yet another failure of a zed drive unit. Hilary wrote to say that D.2-003 was now afloat, with trials due to start on 10th February. On the 'down side', Malcolm had left for John Brown's and John Orr and others from the

Fibreglass Shed were about to go. He, Hilary, was trying to make his mind up whether to go to Vosper's or "stay with the sinking hovercraft". The Author still has the correspondence received from this time onwards and this, together with diary notes and newspaper cuttings, is the basis for the story to follow.

To return to Hilary: The Liquidator had offered him a six month contract with the task of converting the D.2 craft to propulsion by line shafting with propellers mounted below the sidewalls. It was clear to everyone, as it must be to the reader by this time, that the reliability of the zed drive propulsion system was so poor that the existing D.2 craft had no sales prospects unless this major defect was rectified. This was also a matter that would discourage any potential buyer of Denny Hovercraft Ltd.; and the Liquidators were in discussion at this time with Short Brothers and Harland of Belfast, who were showing interest. There was also news from Hilary that he had visited the "Barrovians", the former DHL staff who were now at the Vickers' shipyard at Barrow-in-Furness and had had a long talk with Charles Morris, who was still very bitter about what had happened and who told "a sad tale of the trouble and strife in the Denny Board Room", and about how "the present plight of DHL need not have come about if the Hierarchy of Wm. Denny Bros. had been of finer mettle, or better still, if they had kept their noses out of the Hovercraft business, and left it entirely, i.e. Technical and Commercial aspects of the job, to properly appointed DHL staff"! In including these statements in this account of the Denny Hovercraft story it is probably just as well that it is now 50 years since the events described. It is a pity that the Board Minutes are not available to trace more sides of the story, but these little clues do add to the picture of what happened.

The next letter was from Ted, including an invitation to visit him at his home, and with more tales of zed drive trouble on D.2-002 and an expression of his low opinion of the unit's hydrodynamics. On the bright side, Hilary reported that D.2-003 had reached 26.09 knots in the light condition with the engines running at 2000 rpm. Clearly Hilary had thrown caution to the winds and had had the craft running at a speed that would have made the zed drive endurance question even worse. But why not 'go for broke'? There was nothing to lose and this was the highest speed recorded by a D.2. to date. How this was achieved is not certain, but Hilary had had fairings, albeit crude but the best that could be made in the circumstances, fitted to 003's zed drives, so this may be the reason for the extra speed. In the same letter Hilary said that he had decided to stay with DHL "to the end". The task that lay before him in totally changing the D.2 propulsion system was a daunting one. In a later letter, Peter Macdonald wrote that this was "a job that I would have boggled at with the whole office to help. For him, I reckon it's damn near impossible".

On the 27th February, 1964, the last of the 'Denny boats' to be launched, Yard Number 1504, went down the slip and became the 11,000 ton cargo vessel *Melbrook*. In the report in the *Daily Express* of 28th February it was said that "only 40 workers were left by the slipway to mourn the silence - and the memories". The ship was taken up-river to be finished at the Alexander Stephens yard.

Early in March the Author visited Ted Tattersall at his house in Hythe and met his colleague Dave Nicholas. There was a showing of the Denny Hovercraft film and we talked sidewall craft all day. This was the formation of a small study group led by Ted with the aim of advancing the design and, if possible, the construction of a future sidewall craft. On the basis of a lot of theoretical studies he had carried out, Ted in particular was totally convinced that there was a market for sidewall Hovercraft which could compete effectively with other forms of high speed craft such as hydrofoil boats.

On 8th May *The Daily Telegraph* reported that a hydrofoil boat had crossed the Channel in 53 minutes and on 20th May *The Daily Herald* had an extensive piece on 'The Race between Hovercraft and Hydrofoils'. Probably the European front runner in the hydrofoil field was the Italian firm of Supramar, with its PT 50 boats. A new company, Condor Ltd., had been formed to operate a PT 50 between St. Malo in France and the Channel Isles. The 91½ ft. long PT 50 was delivered, making what *The Daily Telegraph* described as a "marathon voyage for such a craft, coming under its own power from Sicily", where it was built. The Author was able to sample the St. Malo - St. Helier return trip in September 1964 and experienced a surprisingly rough ride over what appeared to be a quite low sea state, with an estimated significant wave height of only about 2 feet.

The Russians were also very active in hydrofoil development, initially for use on their river systems and later sold to other areas, such as the more sheltered parts of the Mediterranean Sea.

According to Ted Tattersall, to be competitive, the cost of the sidewall Hovercraft would have to be no more than £3000 to £4000 per un-laden ton (At 1964 prices of course).

For comparison, the costs attributed to the Denny craft in 1963 were as follows:-

D.2-001 (prior to accident), £75,000

D.2-002 including all trials and considerable modifications to the propulsion system, £113,000

D.2-003 to completion, estimated to be £82,000 (About £4100 per un-laden ton)

It was also estimated that if the D.2 craft were built in a new factory with design modifications to allow the craft to be assembled in larger pieces and with the canopy over the passengers in GRP instead of the aluminium framed and glazed structure, the build cost could have been reduced to about £57,000 (About £2900 per un-laden ton). This point about the canopy being in GRP is important since this is what was done on the later HM.2.

For a time there was a degree of optimism from Hilary following a Hovercraft Development Ltd./ Denny Hovercraft Ltd. meeting in London, with the main conclusion that the propulsion problem had to be dealt with.

At South Marston only a small team was active on Hovercraft and, with work getting light, a group of five stress engineers under the Assistant Chief Stress Engineer Alistair Mackay was sent to the

British Aircraft Corporation factory at Filton in Bristol to pick up some stressing sub-contract work. At the time Filton was very heavily committed to Concord (No 'e' on the end yet) and was losing people every week to Boeing and the American supersonic transport programme. Our group was in a hotel in Bristol for a little over a week before returning home with work packages covering fatigue records for the Bristol Britannia and a substantial amount of stressing on the rear of the BAC 1-11 airliner. As time went by the work packages extended to some tricky work on Concord and to other studies for the Atomic Energy Research Establishment (AERE) at Harwell. From time to time there was some Hovercraft work, on VA-4 and a proposal for a craft with an inflated flexible side structure, but this was very sporadic. So that was the 'day job' that developed and continued through 1964 and 1965.

In the evenings and week-ends the Author did what he could to answer the steadily increasing bombardment of questions from Ted on the structures of the sidewall Hovercraft projects on which he and Dave Nicholas were working in their 'spare' time, and occasionally drove at week-ends to Ted's house in Hythe for project meetings. No money was yet available to build the craft, so to have any hope of success it had to be small. Unfortunately, the bigger they are the better they work.

Despite the condition Denny Hovercraft was in as a company Denny still held the licence for sidewall Hovercraft. So in September 1964 Hilary went to HDL at Hythe to discuss new flexible skirts and fan ducts for the D.2s. The Dumbarton office was to be closed in October, when Hilary would move to London as official manager of the project and to get closer to the work on D.2-002 at the Thames Launches yard on Eel Pie Island. The project was still being supported by the joint liquidators of William Denny and Brothers, and it was reported in *Engineering News* in November 1964 that it was their assessment that the chances of selling Denny Hovercraft Ltd. were sufficiently real to warrant the expenditure of no more than £20,000 for the purpose of modifying the propulsion systems of the D.2-002 and D.2-003 craft.

The general situations described above continued to the end of 1964 and the first months of 1965 when Government cancellation of the TSR2 project in April sent shock waves through the aircraft industry and beyond, with knock-on effects at Vickers at South Marston which had been contracted to manufacture parts of the aircraft. Jigs and fixtures waiting for use in one of the hangars were ordered to be destroyed, immediately. The cancellation decision had been taken and there was to be no possibility of reviving the project.

Hilary had now reached the stage of having a design for an alternative propulsion system for D.2-002 and D.2-003. His drawings showed the propulsion engines turned round so that their output drive shafts pointed forward, instead of aft as they had been originally. This allowed the original support structures for the engines to be used with little or no modification. Two Reynolds triplex chain drives ran from the port engine to the port sidewall, where the chains meshed with sprockets on a gear box that had an inclined output shaft that pointed aft and lined up with the shaft driving the port propeller. There was a similar arrangement on the starboard side. Thus both propellers were mounted behind the sidewalls, minimising, it was hoped, the problem with hitting driftwood, and eliminating the zed drive issue.

In May Ted and Hilary met with a possible financial backer, 'Mr. X', for the small Hovercraft that had been the subject of the studies by the little group that had worked at week-ends and in evenings since early in 1964. Things were starting to look up, and pressure to get on with the various aspects of the design and other work intensified. One part that had the Author 'scratching his head' was the bow of what had now emerged as a glass reinforced plastic hull - with a vee bow of course, taking account of the lessons from D.2 and the ideas kicked around the DHL office at Dumbarton. Assessing the strength required to withstand local water impact pressures was easy enough, but working out how the total load on the bow was passed back into the main hull was the problem. If Finite Element Methods had been available, as they are today, there would have been no difficulty, but in the mid 1960s the slide rule was the primary, and in our case, the only means of calculation, together with a lot of imagination in the mind of the stress engineer.

To help the visualisation process the writer decided to make a card board model of the bow. Then, why not use balsa wood - it would be easier to work with? And if the bow was the most complex part, it would not take much more effort to make the complete hull. The end result was a complete model, with an HDL fingered bow skirt of course, that proved useful in ways never imagined at the outset.

The first picture below was taken at Ted's house in Hythe, with Dave Nicholas on the left, Ted in the middle, the Author (Age 30) on the right, and Ted's boys Nicholas and Adrian. The model was then taken to a pond near Beaulieu and floated on a piece of polystyrene for photographs

So the primary use of the model, which the Author still has, was in promotion of the project and in discussions with potential backers and clients. Hovermarine Ltd. was formed secretly in late September/early October 1965, and letters from Ted started coming with the Hovermarine letterhead instead of the variety of pieces of paper used previously.

At Eel Pie Island, Hilary was still struggling on with modifying D.2-002, and described his feelings by saying that he "would never undertake such a task again without competent assistance as at times I feel the job is too much for me. However I am getting it done but feel that the cheeseparing of our account friends is proving a false economy". The main changes to the craft involved the new propulsion system with its chain drive, constant velocity joint, stern tube, thrust blocks, shafting, propellers and rudders; sheathing the craft bottom with glass reinforced plastic; replacing and remounting the canopy; extending the sidewalls and fitting HDL type flexible skirts. This appears to have been a much more extensive programme than originally envisaged by the Liquidators. Approval of all this work had to be given by the A.R.B. - the "Arabs" in Hilary terminology - who would not allow any mechanical fixing of the sidewall extensions in case the water-tightness of the sidewalls was compromised. The extensions had to be bonded to the original sidewalls. Even the experts consulted by Hilary were uncertain about the integrity of this arrangement. He summed up the situation by saying "It is all one problem after another, made doubly difficult by the fact that it is not enough to draw things on paper and give them to the yard. Unless you have people brought up in the way of all this kind of work and brought up to think things out just a little for themselves - in other words a set-up like Dick Hartley and John Orr with a band of trusty laminators and a few Bixies thrown in to do the mechanics - unless you have this you just have to go out in the yard and roll up your sleeves and spell it all out by example".

On October 7th, 1965, at his house called *Tighnabruaich* in Ulverston, C.F. Morris penned a letter to *The Scotsman*, responding to an article in that paper on 28 September on Hovercraft on the Clyde, which described the journey of Denny's Hovercraft to London as "ill-fated" and said that it was the Hovercraft project that had "helped to ruin the company". Morris responded as follows, referring to the D.2 craft:

"This craft was to be made in glass-reinforced plastic. In the opinion of the Board of William Denny, this craft could not be produced quickly enough and therefore a wooden prototype was made. This was the craft mentioned in your article as the one which 'helped to ruin the company'.

The D.2 hoverbus, as it was called, was designed to operate in smooth water conditions to be found on rivers, lakes and in sheltered coastal waters. At the time she was built, the glass-reinforced plastic mouldings were the largest produced in this country and, perhaps, the world.

Also, at that time, she was the only hovercraft that was absolutely seaworthy and 'quiet in operation' and which could compete commercially with any other known form of water transport as a passenger or passenger/car ferry. Most of these facts are probably still true today. The first D.2 hoverbus built in glass-reinforced plastic journeyed in May 1963 some hundreds of miles unaccompanied through open and, at times, very rough seas from Dumbarton to London. There were difficulties which were almost entirely due to the propulsion units and natural hazards such as fog and storms - in other words the troubles were not 'hovercraft troubles' but those of any fast marine craft driven by high-speed water screws. The journey of D.2 should have been hailed as a triumph instead of an ill fated journey".

A very positive report on Hilary's work to modify D.2-002 appeared in *The Scotsman* of November 19, 1965, under the title 'The Phoenix on Eel Pie Island'. The article described completion of the craft modifications described above and announced the imminent return of the craft to the water. A maximum speed of 30 knots and a cruising speed of 25 knots were predicted. It was also observed that a satisfactory outcome to the sea trials would improve the outlook for the Denny stockholders. So Hilary's work to rescue Denny Hovercraft Ltd. was almost complete and he became progressively more involved in what was going on at the infant Hovermarine Ltd., mainly on the small Hovercraft known initially as the 30 seat craft but now HM.1 - Hovermarine 1.

In December Hovermarine went public with the announcement that the company would work in association with Denny Hovercraft Ltd. to develop sidewall air cushion vehicles and the press release described a family of craft extending from 30 seats to 150 seats. Bearing in mind the

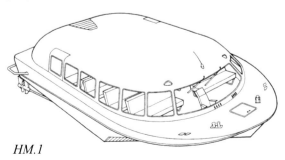

HM.1

almost non-existence of Denny Hovercraft Ltd. in practical as opposed to legal terms this arrangement may seem rather strange. The reason for it was that Denny Hovercraft Ltd., apparently, still held the licence to design and build sidewall craft and Hovermarine did not have a licence. It took until February 1967 for Hovermarine to be awarded its licence and for the way ahead to be cleared for the production of the firm's first craft - the HM.2. Effort was concentrated on the HM.2 and it was announced in December 1967 that the first craft was due for trials.

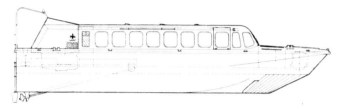

Hovermarine HM.2

These trials were successful and a company press release of February 1968 had the heading 'FIRST HM.2 TO ENTER SERVICE SHORTLY   BRITAIN'S WORLD BEATER'. The press release also listed details of the Hovermarine Board: Managing Director N.D. Piper; Commercial, Production and Sales Director G.C.J. Hodgson; Technical Director E.G. Tattersall; Financial Director J.D.C. Stone and Engineering Director H.M. Watson. Hilary had well and truly earned his spurs!

On a bleaker front, the Vickers Hovercraft team was to be made redundant or 're-deployed'. The background to this was that in February 1966 the greater part of the British Hovercraft industry was merged into a single corporation, to be known as the British Hovercraft Corporation (BHC). This was a political decision with aspects that upset Christopher Cockerell to the extent that he resigned from Hovercraft Development Ltd. It was unrealistic to expect both the Westland SR.N4 and Vickers VA-4 projects to go ahead. So the Vickers project was cancelled and the Vickers Hovercraft group moved to Southampton to be set to work on the SR.N4, which kept the engineers and designers very busy until the demand for assistance on the SR.N4 project ran down, as always happens on projects, particularly big ones. Then the redundancies started.

On the personal front, the Author had come to the conclusion early in 1966 that it was necessary to put family responsibilities higher up the priority list and to find a more stable employment. The preference would have been to leave Vickers and join Hovermarine but this would have been very difficult financially. So with great reluctance a letter of resignation was handed to Vickers just before the merger and formation of the British Hovercraft Corporation. Involvement with Hovermarine on a correspondence basis continued for some time but eventually became a trickle as we went our separate ways. As things turned out the decision meant that the Author avoided a few 'shipwrecks'. But it was a wrench to cease working on these very interesting projects.

What happened at Hovermarine is described in Ted Tattersall's own words in Chapter 9, and the Denny Hovercraft story continues in Chapter 11.

Chapter 9

The story of Hovermarine

What follows here is the second part of Ted Tattersall's lecture to the Newcomen Society in Birmingham on 1st November, 2000. The text is repeated almost exactly as Ted sent it to the Author, who has assumed that there would have been pictures, probably in the form of 35mm slides, to accompany the text when the lecture was presented. Since these pictures were not received with the text the Author has taken the liberty of inserting some illustrations, all except one being from Hovermarine, sent by Ted to the Author during the years following the formal setting-up of the Company.

The story of Hovermarine is presented here to give full credit to those who strove to make sidewall Hovercraft a commercial success, and to extend the story of the design and manufacture of sidewall craft to its U.K. conclusion; and perhaps to give clues to what the future might have held for Denny Hovercraft Ltd., had the Dumbarton company continued as a truly 'going concern'.

This is Ted's story:
"The Board of Denny's decided to build a passenger river-craft the D2, which accommodated about 80 passengers at speeds of 20 to 25 knots. This vessel operated for some time on the Thames between Greenwich and Westminster after being delivered under its own power through the Scottish canals and down the East Coast in 1963! Three of these craft were built when sadly in 1963 Denny's went into voluntary liquidation based on a lack of orders for their 'bread and butter' ferry designs.

As a result my team at HDL were gradually disbanded as most emphasis and financial support went on the amphibious hovercraft and in particular the 200-ton SRN4 project. We had acquired by then considerable model testing data on sidewall hovercraft operating at much higher speeds than contemplated by Denny's.

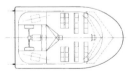

I maintained contact with some of the engineers at Denny's and with a couple of members of my team at HDL, formed an external study group which met at my home at weekends to try and put together an outline design for a small craft which might interest an operator or investor.

After several months only one ex-Denny's engineer was able to continue and it seemed that the project was going to fade away when an opportunity presented itself. Two commercially experienced gentlemen, then working at Hawker Siddeley, with some experience working in the high-speed marine business, visited HDL and asked to be briefed on the potential merits of sidewall hovercraft as perhaps they personally might be able to resurrect or buy the Denny designs. At the end of this discussion it was obvious that they were pretty enthusiastic and we agreed to meet again away from HDL. A few months later these two gentlemen, Norman Piper and Gerald Hodson together with our accountant Jim Stone, the one engineer from Denny's Hilary Watson and myself became the founding members of Hovermarine Ltd in September 1965. We had little or no cash; between ourselves we raised about £1500. We had no other capital.

Of course I had to leave the relative security of HDL. Christopher Cockerell was deeply concerned about my welfare and that of my young family and the Board of HDL were absolutely livid! As I pointed out to Christopher, I was only continuing what I had promised him to do and that was to 'Champion' as he put it the cause of the sidewall concept and I realised it was going to be rough at times. I wholly believed in the validity and competitiveness of this version of the hovercraft. The HDL Board was keen not to detract from their main decision to back the amphibious hovercraft and in particular the SRN4. I managed to procure a small study contract with the Ministry of Aviation, which allowed me to work full time as well as assist the others in hunting for sources of investment. This was made considerably more difficult because HDL wouldn't contemplate consideration of a licence to use the hovercraft portfolio to which I had contributed several patents, without a substantial bank balance, and investors were reluctant to consider investment without the licence and with little enthusiasm on HDL/NRDC's part to further the sidewall project.

Gradually a brochure of outlined designs and a reasonable business plan was put together with very valuable help from the Technical Publication and Marketing Dept of BP UK and in Holland with presentation and printing. However by the spring of 1966 funds became very depleted. The Hovermarine members decided to make a last ditch effort by exhibiting at the 1966 Hovershow which took place near Gosport. Here a contact was made with the Personal Assistant to the chairman of Czarnikow Ltd., a leading firm of commodity brokers - the PA was ex-Royal Navy and enthusiastic about high speed craft. He recommended to his Chairman to invest in this embryonic company and Czarnikow agreed to invest £50,000 in Hovermarine against the firm securing orders for at least two craft. We soon collected a strong design team but it took a further six months to negotiate a licence from NRDC and the HDL Board.

The design team concentrated its efforts on a 60 passenger craft, the HM2, whose specification had been derived from previous market surveys which centred around the three most important

considerations - how big should it be? - how fast should it operate? - can it be produced at an economic price? The craft had to be large enough to offer a reasonable level of ride comfort in the seas it was most likely to operate in. Its speed must be appropriate to the traffic potential and frequency of service. It had to be sold at a price that would enable the operator to make a profit. Considering inshore, estuarine and island routes a vessel in the region of 16 to 18 metres seemed satisfactory for operation on up to 95% of occasions; the craft would carry 60 to 80 passengers and have an operational speed of 30 to

35 knots. But how could we contain the cost to make it attractive. We were selling in the main to existing ferryboat operators who employed marine engineers with craft driven by Master Mariners. Although we could have achieved very low structural weight with light alloy techniques derived from the aircraft industry, it would have been inordinately expensive and so we chose fibreglass as the structural material. Although somewhat in its infancy as a stressed skin type of construction it had already been introduced to the

marine industry and the basic maintenance skills were there. Again, although gas turbines were much lighter they were extremely fuel thirsty at the size we had to consider and again very expensive. And so from the start, we chose high-speed water-cooled diesel engines.

Hovermarine couldn't afford to set up its own construction facilities, so it depended on subcontract facilities. The prototype hull was towed to Hovermarine's fit out and trial base on the River Itchen in Southampton in December 1967 and it hovered for the first time in the early spring of 1968.

In parallel with the hull build, a number of research programmes on scale models were undertaken which checked out performance, handling and stability characteristics. We derived suitable skirt configurations at the bow and the stern. We developed a unique angled rudder system that ensured the craft banked into turns and which later on proved to be  appropriate for application to a unique roll control system. Hovermarine sold the prototype to British Rail Hovercraft on March 25th 1968 but the company was only too aware of the problems of putting the prototype into commercial service so soon.

We had approached the Ministry of Technology a year earlier to buy the prototype for protracted evaluation - The Ministry declined, stating they preferred "to see whether it works first". The craft operated between Ryde and Portsmouth Harbour and there was a number of system failures mainly to do with the developing skirt and the propulsion machinery. The craft performed extremely well however and proved its overall fuel efficiency. Everybody in the company worked long hours to correct the problems, which sapped a lot of the company's resources. Craft began to be sold overseas - we worked with Decca Navigator to produce a high-speed hydrographic survey craft - one of these was sold to a company from Pakistan and another craft was sold to Bombay. This craft experienced fan problems and a somewhat irate customer expressed their concern via our embassy who passed the complaint back via the Ministry of Technology in London. This spurred the Ministry into action and they agreed to purchase the 10th craft for evaluation by the National Physical Laboratory. But by then we had in fact built ten prototypes!

In spite of a further injection of capital by William Cory which enabled us to have built our own manufacturing facility, a lack of sufficient orders during 1969 forced Hovermarine into voluntary liquidation on the 5th November.

 Also during 1969, considerable interest in the Surface Effect Ship was growing within the US Navy and many millions of dollars were to be expended on duplicated research programmes with Bell Aerosystems and Aerojet General and the numerous small contractors and subcontractors that joined in. Over this period Hovermarine had met up with a number of these to explore the possibility of an association. One small company, Transportation Technology Inc., showed considerable interest and with the backing of a Texan millionaire decided to buy the assets of Hovermarine and to

continue manufacture in Southampton. I was kept on as Chief Designer and Technical Director. My new American co-directors sold their homes in the States and moved with their families to Southampton. They left a skeleton staff back in the States to work on some small Navy contracts. Of course the company had to build up slowly again as new orders came in. Besides a new injection of capital, the main talent of the American management was their flair in marketing. Over the 1970's a further 80 craft were sold including versions of the HM2 stretched up to 21 metres. The most successful operator was Hong-Kong and Yaumati ferries which purchased 34 craft. These ferried up to eight million passengers a year. Special purpose versions for port patrol and fire fighting were built and sold. Hovermarine customers were literally scattered all over the world.

Over the period 1980-81 Vosper privately purchased the company from the Americans, which allowed us to continue the development of a larger series of sidewall hovercraft, the HM527, a 27 metre long 200 passenger craft. Four of these craft were sold into Hong Kong and still operate today to the outer islands. The team at Vosper Hovermarine received the Queens Award for Exports for 1982/83 and a Design Council award in 1985 for the design of the HM200 and HM500 series. Also during the early eighties, considerable research and design studies were undertaken on what we called the DEEP CUSHION CONCEPT that allowed large craft of 500 tons or more with speeds in excess of 50 knots to have an open water capability. We saw this not only as a considerable step in the concept's ferry potential but also a fast reaction Naval Vessel with a range well in excess of 1000 miles.

But again, after exporting over one hundred HM200 and HM500 series craft, fate and lack of cash flow brought a dramatic end to this enterprise. It became obvious during 1985 that Vosper's resources were dwindling when their other Company in Singapore had to close. Vosper also claimed the Government had not properly compensated it when Vosper-Thornycroft was nationalised and after many years of legal expense it had to accept that no funds were forthcoming. In the spring of 1986 Vosper-Hovermarine was put into the hands of the Receivers. Although the assets were again purchased by another small American group there were not sufficient resources to continue development and no sidewall hovercraft are manufactured in the UK at this time.

As I have already mentioned, Christopher Cockerell was given a knighthood in 1969 for the Hovercraft invention. It was a great privilege for me to work with him and count him as a friend. After he felt he could no longer make any further contribution to the Hovercraft, his mind was continually searching for quantum jumps in other areas of technology. He worked on advanced concepts of mechanical and electronic engineering up to a few months before he died at the age of 86. I sat with him alone for a short while a week before and thanked him for his inspiration and friendship - he responded with his usual exclamation - "Ted, that's amazing!" I think Robert Browning summed up Christopher's attitude to life when he wrote the lines - "A man's reach is further than his grasp, or what's a heaven for?"

And Hovermarine's look to the Future!

Chapter 10

A very brief Note on Flexible Skirts

In his experiments to reduce friction between a boat's hull and the water supporting it, Christopher Cockerell realised, very early on, the importance of having a deep air cushion, so he experimented with a simple punt with extended catamaran side keels and rigid/sprung doors at the bow and stern to form the plenum seal. The results were more encouraging but the end seals were buffeted unacceptably in quite small waves. This led him to his idea of the momentum curtain, the air jet that contains and supplies pressurised air to the cushion. The early picture of SR.N1 in Chapter 3 shows that the gap between the bottom of the craft and the ground is quite small - say about nine inches on average. To operate in a rough sea without serious wave impact on the structure would require much more clearance than this, and more clearance requires more power. The solution followed by Hovercraft designers was to get a degree of containment of the air cushion by means of some form of flexible skirt. In a Westland advertisement on the front cover of the journal *Air Cushion Vehicles* in May 1963 the company described their invention of the Westland-patented skirt, claiming that it gave "out-standing over-wave and obstacle clearance capability". A four foot high skirt was fitted to SR.N1 and published photographs showed quite dramatic obstacle clearing benefits. The pictures below are of a developed Westland skirt fitted to an SR.N6 craft, photographed at Largs on the Clyde coast in 1965.

Looking at the skirt crumpled up and being scuffed on the Largs beach, it is clear that wear would be a significant design and material issue, not only when operating on a beach or ramp or over even rougher and more abrasive surfaces but also due to buffeting as the craft moved at speed over waves. During this same early period the nascent Hovermarine group was also struggling with flexible skirt design, but coming at the issue from a different direction.

During the Author's visit to Hovercraft Development Ltd. in September 1963, mentioned in Chapter 7, the demonstration of the Hovercraft model with a fingered-segmented skirt all round its periphery was an 'eye-opener'. The potential of this invention by Denys Bliss of Hovercraft Development Ltd. was immediately obvious and as soon as possible the Author sketched out was he had seen. This rough sketch is still in the Author's file and is shown below. To try out the fingered arrangement at Dumbarton, where there was a quiet spell, John Orr made a simple sidewall model in the form of a

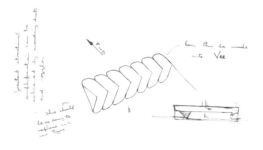

wooden box with an opening on the top for an air supply (from the Author's Hoover) and a slot at the 'aft' end to feed air to the sample of flexible nozzle made for the D.3 test tank model, also given to the Author during the visit to HDL. The reason for this arrangement was that open fingers at the 'aft end' did not seem like a very good idea since on an actual craft moving forward the fingers would scoop water. Fitting the section of D.3 model skirt allowed visual comparison of the two arrangements and also fed air into the model's cushion area. As has been said before, the fingers worked beautifully, admittedly under still water conditions.

There are also some other comments written on the sketch: "This should be as easy to replace as a car tyre" and "Greatest structural simplification can be achieved by avoiding ducts and nozzles". Certainly, it was the case that having a Cockerell style peripheral jet at a craft bow weakened the structure at exactly the place where water impact loads would be greatest. So if feeding the cushion air supply could be achieved in a different way, this could greatly improve the structural design.

The lower part of the page had some tentative thoughts on what an overall arrangement might be. The top sketch had two sets of fingers with a lower pressure than the main cushion pressure between them. On D.2 it had been found necessary for pitch stability reasons to have a transverse skirt. Would this give the same benefit, and would the lower cushion pressure between the skirts soften the bow impact?

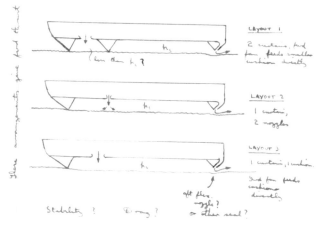

The middle sketch had the cushion partition provided by a transverse air jet, to deal with the stability problem, if there was a problem. The bottom sketch dispensed with the transverse jet and had air blown straight into the cushion.

But all three notions still had the rear flexible skirt with its air jet - not a good feature so something needed to be done about that. When Ted Tattersall got his little week-end and evening group going, the craft that he and Dave Nicholas schemed out - the 30 seater craft, later called HM.1 - appeared as shown over in model form, viewed from underneath. There is a vee bow with a segmented finger skirt and a simple inflated bag across the rear of the craft. This original scheme had air being blown directly into the cushion and inflating the fingers at the bow, like the HDL demonstration model, but with air at a higher pressure being directed to inflate the bag at the stern. (The little white marks are cotton wool used to make the fingers stand up with the model inverted for the photograph.) The vee bow and the fingers can be seen in the picture of a production HM.2, which did not have the plenum arrangement schemed on HM.1.

At this stage in the development it can be observed that the function of the bow skirt is to contain the air cushion and absorb impacts with small waves. Impacts with larger waves would still be taken directly on the bow structure. The next stage was to extend the skirt upwards on a balloon-like inflated structure and to attach the fingers to the bottom of the balloon as shown below. Wave impacts would now fall on the balloon and the fingers, greatly reducing what might otherwise have been very high local impact pressures. The craft would still feel an impact, but in a much less severe and more distributed way. With the balloon-like or inflated-tube arrangement there was now no need for a continuous slot to create Cockerell's momentum curtain. Pressurised air could be fed into the tube at discrete positions and the tube used to duct the air to the fingers or bled directly into the cushion, as the designer required.

Two of the pictures below show a Griffon Hovercraft approaching a beach at Leith on the Firth of Forth. The craft has a large and extensive inflated structure round its periphery, and below the 'balloon' are the segmented fingers. There is a noticeably lower spray level at the bow than on the early craft that depended only or partly on a Cockerell style air jet - compare these pictures with the very early picture of D.2-001 operating off Dumbarton.

The evolution of modern skirt designs did not happen overnight. It required a lot of engineering experimentation with the design and in the development of the materials used for the inflated structures. Air loss from the cushion is greatly reduced, though the small air gap between the fingers and the water does reintroduce some friction with consequent additional drag to be overcome by the propulsion system. It was Cockerell's invention of the peripheral air jet pressurising the air cushion that initiated the Hovercraft industry, but it was the development of the flexible skirt that made the Hovercraft into a practical reality.

Chapter 11

Denny and Norwest Hovercraft

On Saturday September 9, 1967, *The Glasgow Herald* front page headlined the story that a bid had been made for the Denny Hovercraft company, possibly leading to the resumed production of sidewall craft on the Clyde. All that Mr. S. R. Hogg, joint liquidator of William Denny and Brothers Ltd., and chairman of the Hovercraft company, would admit was that negotiations were going on and nothing had been signed so far. The article went on to say that three Denny D.2 craft had been built (tactfully omitting D.2-001) and that two of them were lying in an uncompleted condition in Clyde boatyards. A brief summary of D.2-002's sightseeing trips on the Thames, said to have been abandoned because of driftwood causing recurrent damage to the propulsion gear, was followed by the statement that a comprehensive modification programme had been carried out, deepening the sidewalls and raising the speed from 17.5 to 25 knots. The craft was at Southampton, had gone through sea trials and was ready for commercial use.

The deal was closed in late October when the joint liquidators sold Denny Hovercraft Ltd. to Mr Frederick Tyrer, managing director of Thomas Fletcher and Co. Ltd. - civil engineers of Mansfield in Nottinghamshire. The agreement was that Denny Hovercraft Ltd. would be sold for about £32,000, with about another £27,000 to be paid to creditors and £5000 for the shares in the company. The deal was subject to a satisfactory response from Hovercraft Development Ltd. regarding the 'sidewall licence' that had been 'purchased' by Denny Hovercraft Ltd.

A more illuminating indication of the situation leading up to the sale was given in the joint liquidators' October, 1967, annual report to the shareholders of William Denny and Brothers. Apparently, "the frustrations and disappointments attending the repair and modification of D.2-002 had been paralleled in negotiations throughout the last year for the sale of the craft or ... the company". The report continued: "Several promising enquiries, involving a very considerable amount of work and discussion, foundered as a result of uncertainty as to the attitude of Hovercraft Development Ltd. to the transfer of the Denny licence to manufacture and sell hovercraft which, it was reported last year, the Government agency were seeking to treat as lapsed or withdrawn".

The Author will interject a few comments here. It would be reasonable to assume that HDL would encourage new entrants to the Hovercraft business, with the intention that revenues would then accrue as these enterprises purchased a licence to use the patents held by HDL and then paid royalties for the use of the patents when craft were sold. The situation appears to have been much more restrictive than this. The Author has on file a note he made on March 8, 1964, while he was with the Vickers Hovercraft Division. The note concerned the period when there were four holders of HDL licences - Vickers, Saunders-Roe, Denny and Samuel White. These companies formed the 'Hovercraft Club'. The note read that "New firms can only be admitted to the 'Hovercraft Club' if members agree. It is probable that no new 'peripheral' members would be admitted. A 'sidewall' member could get in by buying the Denny licence (This is one reason for Denny Hovercraft continuing as a going concern. This licence is a valuable asset.) The Denny licence may lapse, and a new member admitted to start from scratch".

When Denny bought the 'sidewall licence' it was due to last until 1977, so why should it lapse because of the troubles in which Denny Hovercraft Ltd. found itself? Looking back on this note, it seems a very odd arrangement if the intention was to promote the development of a new industry.

Continuing with the extract from the joint liquidators' report: "After many months of negotiation, during which the cost of maintaining the craft continued to mount, the joint liquidators advised Denny Hovercraft Ltd. that no further sums could be advanced to meet either its requirements for current expenditure or to discharge its outstanding creditors of rather less than £27,000. A solution had to be found which would, at least, ensure payment in full to these creditors".

The over-riding impression from the joint liquidators' report is of their frustrations and desperation to get Denny Hovercraft sold, while realising as much as possible of the company assets. Considering what had been spent at Dumbarton on designing and building the D.2 series craft (Probably about £250,000) and subsequently on modifying D.2-002, Mr. Tyrer's purchase price of £32,000 and his commitment to pay an additional £32,000 to clear all debts, seems like a bargain basement price. So what had he purchased?

The obvious assets were the three Hovercraft - D.2-002 which had been extensively modified and, presumably, was ready to go into service; D.2-003 still in storage at McAllister's Dumbarton boatyard and, though having successfully undergone sea trials on the Clyde, still unchanged from using the zed drive units that had been the source of so much trouble and embarrassment to her sister; and D.2-004 which was far from complete and was in storage at a Rosneath yard on the Gareloch.

D.2-003 in storage at McAllister's at Dumbarton

The name Denny Hovercraft Ltd. would continue, and a subsidiary company to be called Norwest Hovercraft with an issued capital in excess of £100,000 would be formed at Barrow-in-Furness, from where two Hovercraft would operate. Mr. Tyrer was quoted in *The Glasgow Herald* (October 24) as saying that he hoped that the three D.2 Hovercraft would go into operation in April (1968) in the Fleetwood to Barrow-in-Furness area, where it was proposed to provide a link between Blackpool and the Lake District. "The two partly finished craft would be taken from the Clyde to Southampton within the next three weeks for completion".

The business of the Hovercraft licence came to a head in May 1968 when the *Scottish Daily Express* reported "**Hover firm sues for £3½ million:** Denny Hovercraft, the Dumbarton firm which built Britain's first rigid sidewall hovercraft, are now claiming damages because they cannot build any more. They have issued a writ against the Government-financed Hovercraft Development Limited, the company holding inventor Christopher Cockerell's master patterns. Denny bought a licence from H.D.L. in 1962 to build rigid sidewall craft, but produced only one completed craft, so in 1965 the licence was withdrawn. The following year the licence was granted to Hovermarine, a Southampton firm who have already sold six of their 60-seater versions of the same type of craft".

It would, of course, be wrong to think that Mr. Tyrer had bought Denny Hovercraft Ltd. in 1967 without having a carefully worked out plan of what he meant to do with the D.2 Hovercraft. As reported years previously in the (Blackpool) *Evening Gazette/ Poulton-le Fylde News* (April 17, 1964), there had been interest in the Isle of Man and Blackpool areas in possible Hovercraft links, with the Westland SR.N4 considered the most suitable type by the Isle of Man Tourist Board. Another news item, about a lecture given in Lytham by R. Stanton-Jones, Chief Designer of Saunders-Roe, to the members of the Preston Branch of the Royal Aeronautical Society, included the statement that Blackpool Corporation had expressed interest in purchasing a Hovercraft to operate round the north-west coast. Also, a feasibility study had recognised the attractiveness of bringing the Blackpool holiday area within quick and easy reach of Barrow-in-Furness, giving access to the very popular Lake District. So some of the basic ground work for introducing Hovercraft had already been done.

No doubt Mr. Tyrer had enthusiasm and good business-like intentions but there were considerable hurdles to cross before having three, or even one, craft available to operate on the proposed routes in the Morecambe Bay area. It was July 1968 before D.2-002 was delivered by Norwest Hovercraft managing director Sir John Onslow from Poole, Dorset, to Fleetwood. This non-stop 550 nautical mile voyage almost completed the circumnavigation of a major part of the U.K. by D.2-002.

The local paper, the *Evening Gazette* of July 8, 1968, greeted the arrival of the D.2 with the headline "Here we are - new lady of the seas at Fleetwood", and showed pictures of the craft painted white and with the name *Denny Enterprise* across the front of the bridge. Almost immediately there was near

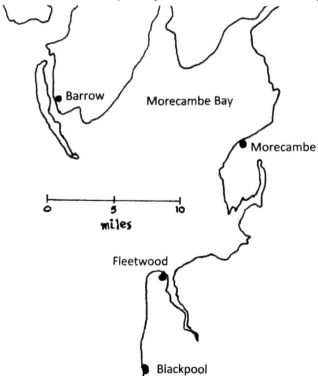

disaster during the night when the craft's pontoon landing stage sank. The craft was taken to safety in the nick of time and it was stated by Sir John that they were going to build a landing stage of a more permanent design, to be ready by the weekend when services to Barrow and Fleetwood were due to begin. The Hovercraft turned out to be Fleetwood's number one attraction and crowds flocked to the pier to inspect her. Progress on starting the planned services turned out to be slower than in the optimistic press announcements, emphasised by a picture in the *Evening Gazette* of July 12 showing the craft on a slipway at Fleetwood for minor repairs.

Denny Enterprise, D.2-002, showing the great reduction in spray from the new bow skirt

Members of the press, including a reporter from *Air Cushion Vehicles*, went on board on July 17 for a pre-inaugural trip from Fleetwood, experiencing a risky transfer to and from the craft that was well below the standard required by the Board of Trade for commercial operations. Once on board, the *ACV* reporter said that "D.2-002 gave a smooth pleasant ride in a 2 - 3 ft. sea in which the accompanying launch was having quite a lively time", but there was adverse comment about the craft being drenched by spray generation. Hovercraft Museum photographs of the craft in operation with its new HDL fingered bow skirt show that spray generation from the bow had been greatly reduced from the time that a pure jetting nozzle had been used. With a 2 - 3 ft. sea running it is likely that craft movement in roll would have caused occasional cushion venting with the associated clouds of spray. There was also mention of the smell of diesel oil from the engines, with the suggestion that this was probably due to journalists and photographers passing between cabin and bridge via the forward engine bay. From the occasions when he was on board D.2-002, the Author has no recollection of diesel smells so the problem was probably due to the reason stated by the journalist. Norwest's plan was for the craft to do 20 return trips between Fleetwood, Morecambe, and Barrow-in-Furness, and for a second craft to be on the route later in the summer.

This second craft could only have been D.2-003, still on the Clyde and delivered to James Adams and Sons (Ship Repairers) at Gourock on July 24 to undergo modifications, presumably to the same standard that Hilary Watson had achieved over many months with craft 002. *The Glasgow Herald* quoted Commander Anthony Gillingham, the Denny Hovercraft managing director, as saying that "they had carried out experimental work with D.2-002, which went into service this week in Morecambe Bay". In fact the 'Abandon Hovercraft' tests on D.2-002 had not yet been carried out to satisfy the Board of Trade so the necessary certificate for operating public services had not been issued, though this was soon rectified with the assistance of 30 junior soldiers from Preston, and finally there was a report in the *Evening Gazette* recording that on August 9 nearly 600 people had experienced 30 minute hover 'flights', with fourteen trips having been operated round Morecombe Bay by 'Fleetwood's Hovercraft'. Sir John Onslow, managing director and chief pilot of Norwest Hovercraft was quoted as saying that "we need a second Hovercraft as soon as possible" and that "the first trips to Barrow would start on Monday (August 12) as scheduled". When the service finally started on August 19 it lasted for only one day before the craft was relegated to carrying out pleasure trips 'around the bay', mainly from Fleetwood. The reason for this decision is unclear but it has been said that the craft was found only to be suitable for these short, 30-minute pleasure trips, not the ferry service planned by the company. The Author can only speculate, and this must be emphasised, that total cancellation of the Barrow run was due to the sea states encountered. Morecambe Bay is very open to the direction of prevailing winds from the south-west and the water depth in the bay shelves significantly towards the north-east. It seems likely that a craft running from Fleetwood or Morecambe towards Barrow would experience more or less beam seas, and possibly choppy seas, on a significant number of occasions, causing frequent venting of the air cushion, spray, and an uncomfortable ride for the passengers. Though the craft had experienced very rough conditions before, these had been with a delivery crew on board, not fare paying passengers.

The next twist in the story was very unexpected, to those watching from the sidelines at least. Denny Hovercraft Ltd. had formed another subsidiary, in Jamaica, called Jamaica Hovercraft Ltd. This subsidiary was going to take delivery of D.2-002 before the end of 1968, with the objective of running the craft between Kingston and the international airport at Palisadoes. D.2s 003 and 004 were still on the Clyde and one of these craft, obviously 003, would take the place of 002 when she went to Jamaica.

As in the case of the Morecambe Bay operation, the 'ground work' had been done some years before. The following summary is from the Jamaican paper *The Daily Gleaner*: Mr. Norman A. Copping, the acting managing director of Jamaica Hovercraft had lived in Jamaica for some 13 years before returning to England. He knew the Kingston area well and, 'while day-dreaming about Jamaica in his London office' in 1965, had the idea of running a Hovercraft across Kingston Harbour to the airport at Palisadoes. It was a natural!! Kingston is situated on a wide bay facing the Caribbean Sea to the south and sheltered from it by a spit of land nearly 10 km long, stretching out to Port Royal at its tip and almost enclosing the bay. About half-way along the spit is the airport. Having been told about Denny Hovercraft, Mr. Copping came to Jamaica and conducted a feasibility study in conjunction with the Minister of Trade and Industry - the Hon. Robert C. Lightbourne - and the Minister of Communications and Works - the Hon. Cleve Lewis. The Cabinet was persuaded to agree in principle to the Hovercraft proposal and in June 1968 a licence was granted to operate a service for a period of five years. The craft was to be called *Humming Bird* since, as Mr. Copping said, "the craft hovers like a humming bird and, of course, it is the national bird of the island".

The craft was due to arrive in Jamaica at the end of November, 1968, and would be operated initially by an English crew that would stay on to train Jamaicans to carry out all aspects of the operation. It was predicted that thirty Jamaicans would be hired. If the traffic justified it, Mr. Copping said that another craft would be brought to Jamaica in 1969.

In due course, in the latter part of 1968, D.2-002, now with the name *Humming Bird* painted across the front of the bridge, was loaded at Liverpool on to a ship bound for Jamaica, not without some problems, since the *Liverpool Echo* reported that the lifting operation had to be postponed when the lifting gear bent (D.2-002 was not fitted with the Denny designed attachment gear).

'Humming Bird' being loaded at Liverpool and the
Hon. Robert Lightbourne going aboard at Kingston

The December 1 issue of the *The Daily Gleaner* had a front page picture of the Hon. Robert Lightbourne going aboard the craft, assisted by an executive of Jamaica Hovercraft. The picture of the event is reproduced here by permission of *The Daily Gleaner*. The accompanying report described how the British-built passenger-carrying Hovercraft, the *Humming Bird*, had arrived in Kingston aboard the Harrison Line Cargo Vessel *Tactician* from Liverpool, England, for the Kingston / Palisadoes service, which would soon be operated by Jamaica Hovercraft Ltd.

As normal with new Hovercraft services there was a trip with local dignitaries and harbour and company representatives, which went well and the craft duly tied up at Port Royal. During the trip the Hon. Robert Lightbourne had taken control for a time. The report stated that the company had plans to extend the service by bringing two more Hovercraft into the operation (D.2-003 and 004?). However, first of all, *Humming Bird* had to undergo certain technical tests in Kingston Harbour and to satisfy the Air Transport Licensing Board before the end of December, before the five year licence could be granted. During these trials the craft ran aground at Sphinx Beacon off Fort Augustus in Kingston harbour, reputedly because the steering gear became defective. The craft was refloated with the assistance of the Harbour Master's boat and later moved to Port Royal under its own power. Underwater inspection of the craft revealed no damage and the vessel's Captain Walker said that the craft had made excellent cruising runs in Kingston harbour since the incident. Another minor problem occurred when the craft had to go in to dry dock 'to change a coupling on its underwater gear', and to install a cooling system to make the craft more comfortable for passengers. By the end of December 1968 it was advertised in *The Daily Gleaner* that the *Humming Bird* would be operating from No. 2 Pier Kingston at regular intervals from 24th December for a tour of the harbour, with tickets obtainable on board at 10 shillings for adults and children half price. The services must have been going well for there were no further reports until 13th May, 1969, when *The Daily Gleaner* reported that the Bustamante Industrial Trade Union was complaining about the Hovercraft service across Kingston Harbour, on the basis that the craft had reduced the earnings of the operators of a limousine service to almost nil. The Union sent a telegram to the Prime Minister on the matter. This was followed by a demonstration by the taxi men outside Jamaica House, with police and soldiers standing by. The demonstrators were reported to have been told that the Prime Minister was considering the issue and would give them word by Monday.

Meanwhile, back in the U.K. work was proceeding on craft 003 while the much less complete 004, still in 'preservation' at Rosneath on the Gareloch, had still to be assembled and 'would be dealt with soon'. The following picture gives an idea of the build state of D.2-004. In this picture the re-designed forward fan ducts and the cabin roof are in position. The forward and rear superstructures, which include the bridge, are not visible and had not been manufactured at this stage. On the last occasion the Author saw craft 004 at about the end of 1963, all fans, fan ducts and the forward and aft fan engines were in place. To be confident of completing the craft, the forward and aft superstructures, at the very least, had to be available. The moulds were necessary to make these from

scratch. So were these moulds also in storage at Rosneath? Alternatively, was it the intention to salvage all the necessary parts from D.2-001? It is unlikely that the answer to this will ever be known, since D.2-004 was never completed. One feature of 004 that has not been mentioned so far is that the propulsion engine support structures were angled so that the zed drive units would have been positioned behind the sidewalls, giving good protection from the drift wood problem. Could this also have been a part of the solution to the short fatigue life of the zed drive units, perhaps by fitting units with a greater power capacity? Regrettably, this can be no more than speculation.

Denny Hovercraft Ltd. announcements said that the company still wished to develop sidewall craft and to this end it was looking at potential Hovercraft construction sites, possibly in Scotland, Wales, Isle of Man or even Malta (*The Glasgow Herald* April 4, 1969). With work completed on D.2-003 at the boatyard of James Adam and Sons at Cardwell Bay at Gourock the craft went on trials. *The Daily Telegraph* (July 16, 1969) reported that the long blue-and-white(sic) craft had been seen daily on the Firth, accompanied by a speedboat bearing the name 'Northwest Hovercraft'. Mr. Frederick Tyrer, chairman of Denny Hovercraft and of Thomas Fletcher, told a *Telegraph* reporter that they hoped that D.2-003 would be a most successful craft, re-engined and fitted with a completely new propulsion system that would give a speed of 28 knots. After about another two weeks on trial, the craft would be inspected by the Air Registration Board. If the ARB and the Board of Trade were satisfied, the craft would immediately be put to work. He also mentioned that another craft of this type (D.2-002) was working successfully in Jamaica, and that there were plans to take over a small shipyard in the UK for the building and maintenance of Hovercraft.

Following completion of the Clyde trials D.2-003 made the journey to Fleetwood, where the picture shows a very smart-looking D2-003 in the late summer of 1969. In September, 1969, the craft made a brief visit to the Langton Graving Dock in Liverpool before returning to Fleetwood.

Since her sister craft had proved unsuitable for open sea work (The D.2s had never been

designed for open sea work.) Norwest Hovercraft Ltd. chartered the ferry *Stella Marina* to run summer services between Fleetwood and Douglas, Isle of Man in 1969.

The Author has no detailed knowledge of what happened to Jamaica Hovercraft Ltd. after the incident with the taxi drivers, except that it was reported in *The Sunday Gleaner* of December 6, 1970, that the Jamaica Hovercraft company had gone bankrupt in 1969 and that the *Humming Bird*, now at its moorings at Morgan's Harbour Marina, Port Royal, had been put up for sale by the Trustee in Bankruptcy.

According to information obtained via Blackpool Public Library, the Norwest Hovercraft terminal at Fleetwood was closed in 1970 and the company went into liquidation in 1971.

From time to time little tantalising items of information, or misinformation, were found about the D.2s, but nothing that could be confirmed with the necessary certainty until Warwick Jacobs of the Hovercraft Museum put the Author in contact with Ken Pemberton of the Hovermail Collectors Club. Until very recently this club published a newsletter called *Slipstream* and Ken has gone through his own records and the last 25 years of *Slipstream*, with the following results:

This February 1972 photograph (Copyright Fast Ferry international) shows D.2-003 on the Thames and claimed to be owned by 'Norwest Ferries', available for sale and with the hull repainted. The next report was of the craft, named *Sortilege*, being operated by Casa Navi SpA of Trieste, on a passenger service between Trieste and Lignano Sabbiadoro at the head of the Adriatic, for a short time in September/October, 1972. After a period with a local nautical school the craft was back in service in July 1973, but "rumour has it" that it was damaged by running aground, to the extent that it was declared at write-off and may have been converted to a restaurant, floating or otherwise (*Slipstream*, May to November 1973).

An issue that perplexed the Author for a while was a set of photographs, from the *Hovercraft Museum*, of D.2-002 in a very bad condition in an unknown boatyard, and still with the Jamaican

flag painted on the side of the craft's bridge, and another photograph, obviously taken later, labelled 'Florida' and with all designations painted over. Ken Pemberton came to the rescue again and this is the outline of what happened to dear old D.2-002.

The picture of 002 <u>was</u> taken in Florida, in 1996. Yes, 1996, thirty-three years after the craft was first lowered onto the water at Denny's Leven shipyard!

The location is off the west side of the Key of Islamorada in the State of Florida. Even if somewhat scuffed and sad-looking and without its D.2-002 insignia, the craft is shown still afloat.

Other items from *Slipstream* tell something of the various adventures and owners of D.2-002 from the time that Jamaica Hovercraft Ltd. became bankrupt. The craft passed through the hands of two or more owners, one having decided to sail the craft to Canada by way of the Intracoastal Waterway that gives a 3000 mile long sheltered route up the east coast of the United States. An outline of what happened was given in a letter from Dennis Daly to *Hovernews*, the newsletter of the Hoverclub of America. Published in the March/April 1992 issue, the story told by Dennis Daly is as follows:

"While on her way to Canada, up the Intercoastal Waterway, in the 70s, she sank! It happens to the best of them. (Author interjection: How this could have happened when the hull had so many sub-divisions is unclear.) After the lawyers and insurance companies had finished screaming at each other, I raised her, converted her and lived on board here in N. Carolina until 1986. We repowered her with maneuvering thrusters. Nine hundred and eighty miles and four months later we arrived at her new mooring at Islamorado in the Florida Keys. Great trip.

Anyway this was only to say, we have a lot of background and pictures of this sidewaller. If there is any interest, I'll dig it out and send you a story."

Regrettably, the Author has been unable to contact Dennis Daly, even though given an address by *Hovernews* Editor Dave Galka, and nothing further was printed in *Hovernews*.

What happened to D.2s 002 and 003 after the events described above is unknown to the Author, but glass reinforced plastic is very difficult to destroy and it is more than likely that the craft still exist in some form, somewhere, fifty years on from the heady days with Denny Hovercraft Ltd. in the Leven shipyard at Dumbarton. And it is not beyond imagination that the sisters are still being used and cared for by owners with a taste for 'classic' Hovercraft.

Chapter 12

Other Hovercraft on the Clyde

This Chapter was written originally as an Appendix since it did not, at first, seem to relate closely to the main themes of this book. As it developed, however, it became apparent that it did link with other Chapters in describing another two attempted commercial operations with Hovercraft in the early days. For in comparison with many other new transport developments, these were very early days. So the message, if there is one, is of the importance of matching the craft to the proposed routes. Also, the Chapter added a little to the Hovermarine story by describing what happened on the Firth of Clyde. In a different part of the world, Hong Kong, the Hovermarine craft were very successful, described by Ashley Hollebone as "an equally familiar sight in Hong Kong as the red Routemaster bus was in London for thirty years", and ferrying up to eight million passengers a year according to Ted Tattersall.

Clyde Hover Ferries and the SR.N6 operation: In March 1965 a contract for the lease of two SR.N6 Hovercraft valued at £100,000 each was signed between Westland Aircraft Ltd. and Highland Engineering Ltd., the parent company of Clyde Hover Ferries Ltd. Clyde Hover Ferries had been set up by Peter Kaye, a businessman and entrepreneur with a remarkably wide range of interests, including a boat yard and chandlers at the very popular yachting port of Tarbert on Loch Fyne, ownership of the Little Cumbrae island and its farm plus ancient castle and with a light house, just off the Ayrshire coast, as well as involvement in construction projects and computer services. From his farm on Wee Cumbrae, as it is known to the locals, Kaye observed the ferry services on the Firth of Clyde and came to the conclusion that something faster than the existing vessels was required to improve communications in the area. This was in the period when Hovercraft were very new and exciting and were predicted to make a significant contribution to transport links. So Clyde Hover Ferries became the prospective operators of SR.N6-010 and 012, and advertised in the press for a manager, pilots, engineers and hostesses, with the intention that the Hovercraft service would start in June, 1965. It was intended to be an all-the-year-round passenger and freight service and it was stated that successful negotiations to accept the craft had been held with the Clyde coast towns of Rothesay on the Isle of Bute, Millport on the Great Cumbrae, Dunoon in Argyll, Gourock, Wemyss Bay and Largs on the east side of the Firth, Helensburgh to the north, Tigh-na-bruaich in the Kyles of Bute and Tarbert on Loch Fyne where the craft would be based. The only refusal was Kilcreggan on the peninsula between Loch Long and the Gareloch, the community being concerned that the competition from the SR.N6s might result in withdrawal of the existing ferry connection with Gourock. The mere list of these names suggests ample scope for developing service connections between the Clyde Coast resorts and the mainland rail-heads at Gourock, Wemyss Bay, Largs and Helensburgh/Craigendoran.

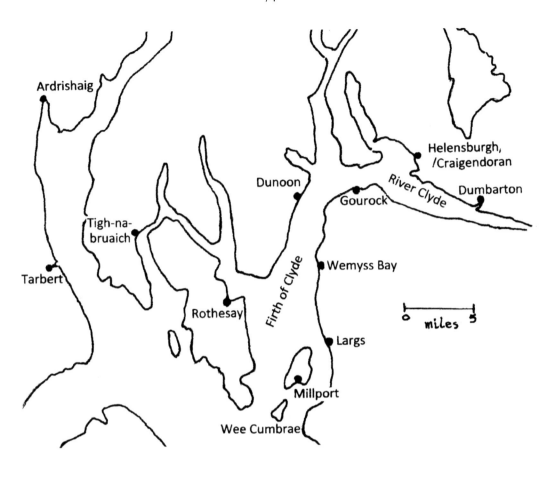

Indeed, in the holiday heyday of the area people came in their thousands to the Clyde Coast resorts, which were serviced by several fleets of steamers. When Peter Kaye decided to introduce his Hovercraft services the ferry and cruising fleet had been reduced to a summer complement of about sixteen vessels - with a mixture of diesel, steam and diesel electric types, of which only four carried cars.

The first of the Clyde Hover Ferries SR.N6s was demonstrated to 250 guests of the company at Finnart on Loch Long on the 18th of June, 1965, the event being reported in *The Scotsman* next day, with a dramatic photograph and under the heading "Craft comes ashore in a shower of spray". Peter Kaye was quoted as saying that the run from Tarbert would be made morning and evening, with tentative services starting to Helensburgh, Gourock and Dunoon. The craft was due to be demonstrated at Largs on the following day. And of course, as so often in these early days in the development of the Hovercraft, there just had to be a problem with the craft resulting in cancellation of the invitations to the Provost and members of the town council, and disappointment for the thousands of trippers who had come to see and experience this new form of transport, and a newspaper headline that read "Hovercraft Just Wouldn't Hover Over Largs".

The scheduled services were advertised as due to start on July 16, as a shuttle service from Largs to Millport and Rothesay. Technically these seem to have proceeded well but later in the year a problem developed at Largs when it was suggested that Clyde Hover Ferries should pay a fee of five shillings per landing for using the beach. Though a small sum in relation to the other costs of running the service, Clyde Hover Ferries thought that their efforts to improve communications should be supported, without the "imposition of additional financial burdens unrelated to any service provided by the local authority" *(Daily Express)*. According to the Council, "boat hirers and everyone who used the beach had to pay something. And the company had agreed to pay British Railways five shillings a call". The result was that on 13th September Largs Town Council agreed unanimously to ban the Hovercraft from Largs beach. Certainly there were complaints from the Largs residents about noise (Airscrews are very noisy devices, over and above any engine noise) but noise did not seem to have been the critical factor. So calls at Largs ceased. Working 16 hours a day as Peter Kaye was while striving to create something new and with long-term economic potential for the whole Clyde area, the Author is inclined to sympathise with Clyde Hover Ferries.

SR.N6 at Largs and approaching the beach at Millport

In early September the craft schedules were extended with one of the two craft leaving Dunoon to link with the 'Blue Train' services, the electric trains, at Craigendoran running to and from Glasgow. Arrangements were also being made to run at night and through the winter, with a searchlight and radar being fitted to each craft.

Another piece of unfortunate news on 10th September *(The Scotsman)* was the accident that had occurred at Gourock when the craft on the new Gourock, Dunoon and Craigendoran route was caught by the wind and thrown against Gourock pier. And the other craft had battery trouble at Rothesay on the Isle of Bute, only becoming operational again when the battery from the damaged craft was taken to it at Rothesay.

A very detailed report on the Clyde Hover Ferries' operation appeared in *The Scotsman* of 28th September, as one of its 'Close-Up' series. The report said that though 60,000 people had travelled on the craft, the company was losing money, £300 in a good week and £1700 in a bad week. Each engine required a major overhaul every 1000 hours, previously 500 hours, and fuel and staff costs were high. The 'keel' (Did the reporter mean skirt?) had a predicted life of 1000 hours but the Clyde units had already been torn twice and Westland had had to station two engineers at Tarbert to do running repairs. It was also stated that a 'Close-Up' reporter had travelled on 27 of the 50 trips the Hovercraft made each day and that on 9 of these there were no passengers. On the rest were 118 passengers, of whom over half were trippers. Probably the key comments were that "Hovercraft are still essentially experimental", and "costing is more or less pure guesswork". The article ended with very positive statements from Peter Kaye, but the future did not look good for the SR.N6 operation. Kaye was not for giving up, planning to reduce fares, and working on the specification for the

Hovercraft that he believed the Clyde needed. The service ceased during the winter of 1965/66. A very much reduced service was offered in 1966 but finished in September, not long before Clyde Hover Ferries Ltd. was placed in liquidation.

Hovermarine on the Firth of Clyde: The development story of the promising Hovermarine HM2 sidewall Hovercraft is described by Ted Tattersall in Chapter 9, including the very regrettable liquidation of the company in 1969. Just prior to this, members of the Scottish Transport Group (STG) had visited Hovermarine due to an interest in developing Hovercraft services on the Clyde. Also in 1969, The Scottish Transport Group, a State owned organisation, took over control of the Caledonian Steam Packet Company (CSPC) from the British Railways Board. So, even though the CSPC was "not over enthusiastic about running such a craft on the Clyde", as observed by Iain C. MacArthur in his fine history of the Caledonian Steam Packet Company, it was the STG that had provisionally booked an HM2 craft, with commuting traffic in mind. Late in 1969 Hovermarine went into voluntary liquidation due to lack of sufficient orders, but was rescued by an American group, with manufacture continuing at Southampton. So, as MacArthur described it, in May 1970 the sidewall Hovercraft HM2-011 arrived at James Watt Dock in Greenock on board the coaster *Saint Agnus*. Initially the craft had to be tested and crew training exercises carried out, and the Air Registration Board had to be satisfied so that a licence could be issued for the craft to 'fly'.

The craft was based at Gourock, where there was good access to fuel and maintenance facilities, and modifications were made as necessary to the piers at which the craft was expected to call. Since the sidewall type of craft was not amphibious like the SR.N6s that had come to the Firth in 1965, it could not run onto beaches and required berthing facilities. Services began in early June and attracted many passengers, for novelty reasons if nothing else, and it was not long before the locals nicknamed the craft the "scooshin cushin".

HM2-011 at Millport pier

When information on the HM2 was first made public in February 1968 the Hovermarine press-release stated that the craft had been "specifically designed for short range operations in sheltered waters". The service routes operated on the Firth of Clyde certainly met the short range criterion but the waters of the Firth can be quite rough at times, even at Largs in the summer season and as far north as the Gourock - Dunoon line, resulting in cancellation of some services in addition to those due to mechanical problems, before the craft was taken into storage at Cardwell Bay for the winter.

HM2-011 on the slip at Gourock

Over the summer period the craft had operated on the Gourock-Largs-Millport-Rothesay-Dunoon routes and had carried 26,000 passengers, but without making a profit. The Company's enthusiasm for the Hovercraft service waned and another attempt at operating air cushion craft on the Clyde came to an end after two summers of operation.

Peter Kaye's vision of a transport network operated by high speed craft was never realised. The fleet of sixteen vessels providing the summer transport and cruising requirements in 1965 steadily reduced in number over the succeeding years, with a progressively increasing emphasis on the efficient transport of cars. The Hovermarine craft became very successful in other parts of the world, showing how important it was to match the craft to the routes operated. In the Firth of Clyde examples good crystal balls would have been useful to help recognise changes of demand due to factors like the popularity of package holidays abroad, increasing use of cars, and the public's preference for day trips to the coast at places like Largs.

Chapter 13

What might have been!

The primary thread running through the narrative in the previous chapters has been the story of the sidewall Hovercraft in the U.K., as told through the experiences of Denny Hovercraft, Norwest Hovercraft, and Hovermarine under its several ownerships. The story started in 1960 and continued until 1986 when Vosper-Hovermarine was put into the hands of the receivers. What might have happened to Denny Hovercraft Ltd. if there had been imaginative financial support for this last of the Denny innovations? Having watched what happened to shipbuilding on the Clyde, when a once great industry almost totally collapsed, there can be little doubt that the William Denny Directors were correct in their assessment of future trading conditions for the yard. But could Denny Hovercraft Ltd. have been at least as successful as Hovermarine, with sales of over 100 HM200 and HM500 series craft in many countries across the globe? The answer to that must be YES, since DHL was already in existence with a skilled and experienced design and manufacturing organisation, and was still actively linked to Hovercraft Development Ltd. at Hythe. The parent company, even if in its last throes, was well known and respected in the shipping world. Contacts are important, as is knowledge of where a product could be sold and operated with advantage to both purchaser and seller. Hovermarine had to build their complete organisation and sales structure from scratch, which they achieved with success, particularly in Hong Kong.

In his 1965 letter to *The Scotsman*, C. F. Morris said that the Hovercraft company was William Denny's only hope, and "If this Elizabethan age had been like the first Elizabethan age some adventurous spirit - - would have backed the Denny venture; but, alas, we all know that this is not a new Elizabethan age and therefore William Denny, a firm of repute, went into liquidation". It is difficult to disagree with this depressing comment. Had sufficient financial backing been forthcoming, Denny Hovercraft Ltd. could have continued at least along the lines of Hovermarine, as a small ship or boat yard. At the end of the Hovermarine story told by Ted Tattersall in Chapter 9, he said that at the present time (Late 2000: Author) no sidewall Hovercraft are being manufactured or operated in the U.K. Would Denny Hovercraft have had a similar history? A possible answer to that question lies in the pages of the highly respected reference volumes published by Jane's Information Group. In 1971-72 Jane's published 'Surface Skimmers: Hovercraft and Hydrofoils'. In the text the Editor commented that "while no-one would suggest that a boom in Hovercraft has begun, or is even just round the corner, there are unmistakable signs that one may not be far away". Details were given of 80 air cushion vehicle manufacturers and design groups active in 17 countries. In the hydrofoil field, 21 organisations in 11 countries were listed.

In the 1987 edition, now titled 'High-Speed Marine Craft and Air Cushion Vehicles', a striking change is that the text now lists an increased number of types of high-speed marine craft - air cushion vehicles and hydrofoils as before, but now joined by high-speed catamaran vessels, wave-piercing hull vessels, semi-submerged catamarans and high-speed mono-hull craft. Hovermarine was given a very favourable mention with sales of "over 100 surface effect ships to 31 countries and is one of the most experienced designers and builders of these craft". Going forward again to the 2009-2010 edition, now titled 'Jane's High-Speed Marine Transportation', the scene has developed even further with eight categories of high speed vessels being designed and built in many countries across the world. Looking across the categories, the number of designs and design variations detailed by Jane's is so great that it is mesmerizing. In some cases a particular design may only have been built as a 'one-off' or in small numbers. From the eight or so countries across the world having commitments to Sidewall or Surface Effect Ships (SES), by far the largest craft is the TSL-A140 *Ogasawara* built by Mitsui of Japan as part of the Techno Super Liner programme. This 140 metre (460 ft.) long, 13,500 tonne craft completed its sea trials in 2005, reaching speeds of over 40 knots in waves up to 2 metres high, but was not accepted by the intended operators since they had come to the conclusion that the operating costs were too high. Looking across the range of sidewall craft, it is noticeable that many have bluff bows, not unlike the Denny D.2. It is clear that bow skirts with HDL type fingers solved the spray problem that required the windscreen wipers on the original D.2 craft to run continuously, and led to the apparent need for craft to have a vee bow.

But for some builders there are construction tables that list large numbers of craft. In the U.K., Griffon Hovercraft Ltd. in particular has 'kept the flag flying' with a very significant number of sales of its amphibious craft. The U.S. Navy has a large number of amphibious 'heavy lift' craft known by the acronym LCAC - Landing Craft Air Cushion - making use of the go-anywhere capability of such craft. For hydrofoil boats the Italian company of Rodriquez Cantieri Navali SpA stands out, and the Russians have built many hydrofoils, but the big success story is that of the Australians with no less than sixteen companies building high-speed catamarans in a complete spectrum of sizes. Two of these companies are world leaders in the design and construction of aluminium vessels. Incat was formed in 1972 and is based in Hobart, Tasmania. In 1990 the Incat catamaran *Hoverspeed Great Britain* was delivered and set a record for the fastest Atlantic crossing by a passenger vessel. Austal, based in Perth, was formed in 1988 and rivals Incat with well over 200 vessels delivered.

The Author's first experience of these catamaran ferries was in the United States, on the service between Boston and Provincetown on Cape Cod. The vessel was the *Salacia*, an Incat design built in the year 2000 by Gladding-Hearn in Somerset, Massachusetts, under licence from Australia. The wake of the ship causes very little disturbance to nearby yachts and the way the vessel manoeuvres at speed and when approaching the landing dock is impressive. With a hull built of aluminium, the vessel has four 2000 HP main engines, each driving a water-jet pump with a 3 ft diameter impeller. It has trim tabs controlled by a gyro and a central computer system, for stabilisation of the ship when under way. It is claimed that this system reduces the vessel motion by 60%.

Travelling on the *Salacia* in the internal accommodation is a pleasant experience, and an exhilarating one out on the fore or after decks, or on the outer top deck.

Salacia is similar in size and performance to the 1963 Denny D.3 project. A tabulated comparison of the D.3 with the *Salacia* is given below.

	Sidewall Hovercraft *The Denny D.3 project*	**Catamaran** *Salacia*
Length (feet)	150 ft (45.7 metres)	145 ft (44.2 metres)
Breadth (feet)	50 ft (15.2 metres)	40 ft (12.2 metres)
All up weight	130 tons	
Passenger capacity	525	610 (417 seated)
Alternative freight capacity	40 tons	
Max. Speed	40 knots in 2.5 ft wave height	39 knots
Cruise speed	35 knots in 4 ft wave height	33 knots
Material	Aluminium alloy	Aluminium alloy
Year built	1963 Denny project	2000
Main engines	Diesels	Diesels
Propulsion engines	2 off, Paxman 12YJC	4 off, Caterpillar 3304
Lift: Forward fan engine	1 off, Paxman 1JHC (?)	None
Lift: Aft fan engine	1 off, Paxman 12YHY	None
Total main engine power	4500 HP (3360 kW)	8000 HP (5970 kW)
Generator capacity		216 kW
Propulsion method	Water screws	Rolls-Royce water jets

The comparisons above suggest strongly that Denny Hovercraft Ltd. and Hovercraft Development Ltd. were on the right track with the D.3 project, with welded aluminium alloy proposed for the structure and the use of marine diesel engines and not gas turbines typical of the large hovercraft of the time. DHL Technical Director Charles Morris had been associated with the liner *Oriana* which used aluminium in its superstructure, which would have been a very useful experience base for the DHL staff, but with still leaving a lot to learn. And the discussions in the office about the pros and cons of water jets should not be forgotten. As projected in 1963 the D.3 sidewall depth was three and a half feet. It is quite possible that the sidewall depth and displacement would have been increased as development proceeded. On the big Saunders-Roe/Westland SR.N4s for example the cushion height was increased eventually to eight feet, giving a very substantial clearance between the craft's hard structure and the sea.

It is tempting to think that, had Denny Hovercraft Ltd. continued in business, development of the ideas in D.3 might have led to something like *Salacia*. Many of the pieces in the jigsaw were there - the need to increase the hard structure clearance while retaining adequate stability, the aluminium structure, the use of marine diesel engines. And the Denny company was already involved with the very successful Denny Brown stabilisers. It is reasonable to expect that stabilising technology would have developed and been applied, perhaps to D.3, almost certainly to later craft.

The cushion air supply on a Hovercraft is a complication affecting the design and first cost of the craft and to some extent the cost of operation, though the anticipated reduction in the overall power requirement relative to the pure catamaran type, as illustrated in the table, might have maintained the balance in favour of the sidewall Hovercraft, especially following the substantial increases in fuel costs that were to come. It is always important for a company to think very clearly about what its objectives are - in this case to build sidewall Hovercraft, or to build fast ferries with no restrictions on the type that might emerge. Reaching the present stage in the optimisation of the fast ferry has taken a long time and a lot of vision and investment, and also required the development of a market for such craft. And there's the rub! When William Denny and Brothers went into liquidation, leaving the orphan Denny Hovercraft Ltd., these things were in short supply. As far as sidewall Hovercraft were concerned it fell to people like Ted Tattersall and David Nicholas, and Hilary Watson with the D.2s, to keep the flame alive until others could join them to produce the HM200 and HM500 series craft. And even that did not in the end prove to be enough.

To answer the question "Why have fast ferries developed?" Andrew Bailey in his November 1997 Paper to the Institution of Engineers and Shipbuilders in Scotland summarised it as follows:

(a)   Demand for fast short range sea transport in areas such as Hong Kong, Australia, the U.K. and Norway.
(b)   The success of early hydrofoils and air cushion vehicles.
(c)   The development of high speed diesel and gas turbine engines.
(d)   The development of the water jet.
(e)   Continuing improvements in the reliability of fast ferry technology.
(f)   The development of regulations.
(g)   Confidence in all-aluminium construction.
(h)   The foresight of a number of ferry operators.
(i)   The "go for it" attitude of the Australian yards.

That just about says it all. Progress is never easy, but progress there has been.

The picture below shows the Incat built P&O ferry *Express* in 2012, slowing down and turning before entering Troon harbour on the Firth of Clyde after a two hour run from Larne in Northern Ireland.

A few years earlier the Author was on a fast ferry leaving Ceuta in North Africa for Algeciras in Spain. Looking down from the rear of the passenger accommodation, it was fascinating to watch the water jet propulsion and steering in operation.

And at Algeciras there was an even more impressive vessel, the Euroferrys *Pacifica*.

Built by the Australian company Austal, *Pacifica* is 101m (331 ft.) long, is built of aluminium, is powered by Caterpillar 3618 diesel engines and is driven by Kamewa water jets. The cruise speed is 37 kts.

Some fifty years earlier these same features were being considered for a Denny sidewall Hovercraft project known as D.3, building on experience gained from the earlier D.1 and D.2 craft.

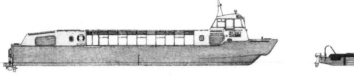

Denny D.2 'Hoverbus' (1963)

Denny Research Craft D.1 (1961)

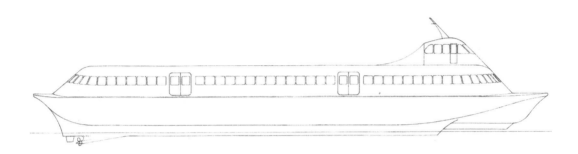

Denny D.3 project

And as for the building capacity of the William Denny and Brothers' Leven shipyard, the last of the 'Denny boats' that went down the slip was the *Melbrook*, No. 1504, 11,000 tons and 523¼ ft. long. Had the Denny projects been allowed to continue it is hard to avoid the thought that vessels like *Salacia*, P&O *Express* and even Euroferrys *Pacifica* could have been built in the yard at Dumbarton.

Why not? Now there's a question.

Postscript to Chapter 13

In 1961 a catamaran model was tested in the Denny Experiment Tank. The opening conclusion in Superintendent Hans Volpich's report was that "The tests of phase 1 of this research programme showed quite promising results at higher speeds".

DUM 1764: Catamaran model tested in the Denny Experiment Tank in 1961

E.H.P. or ¾ m.p.h. in speed. No comparative deadweight figures were available for the two comparative craft. The overall width of the Catamaran Carrier was 62' against 72' for the normal Paddle driven carrier.

6. Conclusions:

(1) The tests of phase 1 of this research programme showed quite promising results at higher speeds;

(2) Should this programme proceed to phase 2, then the resistance qualities of the individual Catamaran form should be investigated. It may be possible to improve the form at lower speeds by the adoption of a spoon bow even if this would mean sacrificing some of the benefits at the higher speeds. This would be of greater importance, if such a Catamaran form would be adopted for a service now contemplated for the Paddle driven Carrier at an operating speed of around 12½ m.p.h. in deep water.

(3) No attempt has been made so far at propulsion Tests. Messrs. B.C.P. should state, whether the adoption of English Electric type 8 SREM Diesels is final, in order to prepare an estimate for tunnel propulsion.

(4) Before making a final decision on the feasibility of this type of craft comparative shallow water tests would have to be carried out, as the picture may change entirely in shallower depths of water.

Superintendent – Denny Experiment Tank.

The document on the left is an extract from Hans Volpich's report of 22nd. November, 1961, on the tests conducted on the ship model numbered DUM 1764, and with William Denny and Brothers, Dumbarton, stamp at the bottom.

References and Bibliography

Air-Cushion Vehicles Originally published as a Supplement to Flight International, later as a journal in its own right. Pub. Iliffe Transport Publications Ltd., London.

The Blackburn: Dumbarton's Aircraft Factory by Alan M Sherry. Pub. Richard Stenlake Publishing, 1996.

The Caledonian Steam Packet Co. Ltd., by Iain C. MacArthur. Pub. The Clyde River Steamer Club, Glasgow, 1971.

Clyde Passenger Steamers from 1812 to 1901, by Captain James Williamson. Pub. James MacLehose and Sons, Glasgow, 1904.

Clyde Shipbuilding Firms. No.1 Messrs. W. Denny and Brothers. The Engineer, Feb. 27, 1891.

The Development of the Saunders-Roe Hovercraft SR-N1 by R Stanton Jones of Saunders-Roe Ltd. Paper presented to the Symposium on Future Developments in Aviation, Cranfield, October 1959.

The Early Days of Hovercraft Development by Ted Tattersall. Lecture given to the Newcomen Society, Birmingham, 1st November 2000.

Fast Ferries - A Transport Revolution? by Andrew Bailey. Paper No. 1564 in the Transactions of the Institution of Engineers and Shipbuilders in Scotland, 11th November 1997.

Fifty Years & More of Hovercraft Development by David R. Lavis, Band Lavis Division of CDI Marine. SNAME and IHS Dinner Meeting, 11 May 2011

High Performance Marine Vessels by Liang Yun and Alan Bliault. Pub. Springer, 2012.

The Hovercraft - A History by Ashley Hollebone. The History Press, Stroud, Gloucestershire, 2012.

Hoverfoil News incorporating Air-Cushion Vehicles from January 1973. Pub. Horizon Publications Ltd., Montacute, Somerset, England.

Janes's Surface Skimmers: Hovercraft and Hydrofoils, 1971-72.

Jane's High-Speed Marine Craft and Air Cushion Vehicles, 1987.

Jane's High-Speed Marine Transportation, 2009-2010. Pub. Jane's Information Group, Coulsdon, Surrey.

King Edward, by Leo Vogt. Pub. The Clyde River Steamer Club, Glasgow, 1992.

Side-wall Hovercraft, by C.F Morris. Paper No. 1274 in the Transactions of the Institution of Engineers and Shipbuilders in Scotland, 19th October, 1962

Slipstream - The newsletter of the Hover Mail Collectors' Club, edited by Ken Pemberton.

Appendix 1

Early beginnings - the first part of Ted Tattersall's Newcomen Lecture

Just as in Chapter 9, this first part of Ted Tattersall's lecture to the Newcomen Society in 2000 is presented here, almost exactly as Ted sent it to the Author.

Naval architecture, as it is still called, had to wait until 1870 when William Froude first put forward the case for a series of model experiments, which on the basis of his speed/length scaling factor, - now appropriately called Froude Number $V/\sqrt{Lg}$ -would be able to determine the resistance of the full scale ship. (He appreciated that the total resistance of a hull was the sum of the wave-making resistance and the skin friction. The latter could be calculated from the results of resistance tests on long thin planks, which would experience negligible wave-making resistance. By subtracting this from the total resistance measured on his models, he could deduce the wave-making drag, which he could then scale up to full size. To this he would add the full-scale skin friction to get the total resistance of the full-scale craft.)

As well as concentrating on the fundamentals of drag analysis, Froude also applied a bit of lateral thinking. One of his more noteworthy considerations was that skin friction might be reduced if air could be bled into the boundary layer of water adjacent to the hull. He was convinced of the potential of this idea to justify making a special model (around 1875) in which he drilled holes in the bottom through which he could feed air under pressure. To his consternation the model resistance increased and as a result he never pursued this line of investigation. What had happened was that he had not blown sufficient air through the system to form anything like a continuous sheet and all he had succeeded in doing was to produce lots of discrete bubbles which effectively increased the relative roughness of the hull surface. Later in 1883 another engineer in Sweden undertook some similar unsuccessful model tests.

At the beginning of the 20th century there were a number of attempts to aerate the bottom of high-speed hulls. The Germans in the First World War tried out a torpedo-launching platform with a forced ventilated step, which continuously leaked air out of the stern. Thornycroft of the Isle of Wight also experimented with a flat-bottomed craft with a semi-rigid leather seal at the bow and with air allowed to escape at the stern. Little or no power saving resulted from these attempts. So, within the boat designing fraternity there was already recognition of the potential of using air as the boundary medium. But until the 1950s nobody had engineered a successful solution.

At that time an engineer with already proven inventive capability had taken the decision to set up an enterprise of his own in the boat building and hiring business. This was Christopher Cockerell. Although initially discouraged by his father, he graduated in engineering at Peterhouse College, Cambridge. He then became a graduate apprentice at W F Allen Ltd the gearbox manufacturers, followed by employment at Marconi's where he contributed significantly to the radio and electronic developments that were so important during the war period. He became a very skilled machinist and enjoyed constructing novel mechanical and electrical devices.

He had sold a very comfortable home and invested all the proceeds in his new business on the Broads, living in a caravan and partly on one of his boats. His enquiring mind soon targeted the performance limits of the hardware he had acquired and, like others before him, he soon became aware of the potential of air lubrication. He modified a small ex-Naval boat by blowing air from a fan out of a slot at the bow - as others had found out negligible benefit resulted.

He soon realised he had to establish a continuous sheet of air (lubrication was not enough). A static deep plenum of air had to be formed under the hull. His next experiment used a simple punt with extended catamaran side keels and rigid/sprung doors at the bow and stern to form the plenum seal. The results were more encouraging but the end seals were buffeted unacceptably in quite small waves. He then took the bold step of substituting the rigid seals by water jets, which to all intents and purposes would be infinitely flexible. He observed how these were bent by the air pressure in the plenum. He then realised that if he used air instead of water in the jets at each end of the punt, they would not only provide the sealing system but also the source of the air which under pressure could lift the hull out of the water.

He modified the model accordingly and it worked straight away. There was a significant reduction on resistance. On further consideration he looked at the longitudinal cross section of the punt and in his mind's eye, rotated this in the horizontal plane about its centre to produce a circular air supported platform - the amphibious hovercraft was born!

The plenum or cushion pressure resulted from the change of momentum of the air jet. In typical Cockerell fashion, he adapted what was immediately available to him to try to quantify what had been discovered. He took two empty tins (Lyons Coffee and Kit-Cat) and located one concentrically inside the other and compared the lift force when a powerful hand held blower was put over a pair of kitchen scales by itself and when attached to the concentric tin device. With the tin device he noticed the lift was augmented several times. He soon deduced that for a given nozzle clearance height, the power into the jet was proportional to the perimeter and therefore the diameter, whereas the lifting capability was proportional to the area of the box and therefore the square of the diameter. So the amount of lift per unit of power to the jet would increase with diameter and that for larger craft for a given hover-height would increase in lift efficiency.

Using this simple jet configuration he built a model powered by an aircraft modeller's diesel engine and demonstrated that this could operate equally well over his lawn and pond. He orientated the jet efflux so that the model was self-propelled and divided the cushion to provide stability.

Christopher had now to quickly find some cash to develop his invention. He tried several big companies including Napier's, de Havilland and English Electric without success. Finally he wrote to Lord Mountbatten who sent a signal down the system and Christopher was asked to demonstrate his model to the Deputy Director of Aircraft Research Mr Ron Shaw and some Admiralty representatives. The Admiralty dismissed it out of hand, but Ron Shaw saw some potential in the idea and asked Christopher if he would be willing to have the idea put on the Secret List so that he could justify looking into it. Shaw eventually contacted Saunders-Roe to vet the idea. Over the eighteen month period that the concept was classified, Saunders-Roe produced a favourable report but the Admiralty still thought the concept ridiculous and that no craft built on the principle would last in a seaway.

Somehow news of Christopher's invention reached Carl Weilland in Switzerland who was also working in this field and he wrote to Christopher to ask if they could work together. Christopher was determined to keep the invention in Great Britain for as long as possible so politely refused. Obviously the invention was no longer secret, so brandishing Weilland's letter he persuaded the MOD to declassify it. This immediately allowed Christopher to approach the National Research and Development Corporation (NRDC). They paid Christopher a nominal sum to assist in the filing of his patents on condition they would have first refusal to purchase his portfolio, which was growing by the day. Even at such an early stage Christopher foresaw the need for flexible skirts.

At this time in 1958 I was just completing a graduate apprenticeship at Saunders-Roe and was spending the last months in the Hydrodynamics Dept that was housed in the same room as the Special Projects Group who were assessing the hovercraft concept. All types of high speed over-water craft were being assessed and some very interesting research was undertaken into planing craft, hydrofoils and further developments on flying boat hull design. Early in 1959 word came around that Cockerell was to set up a small research team at a house about 200 yards from the entrance of Saunders-Roe Head Office. I expressed an interest with a couple of others from the Special Projects group and on March the 1st I was seconded to him after a two-minute interview. His reaction to my expression of interest was "That's amazing! You must be mad!"

Well, NRDC finally agreed, but only through the casting vote of the chairman, to form a research company Hovercraft Development Ltd (HDL) with Christopher owning 25% of the shares and all his hovercraft patents purchased by the company. I then officially left Saunders-Roe and became one of HDL's first employees. Initially we worked in the scullery of The White Cottage, the new home for the Cockerell family. Our working spaces were very limited to say the least. Somehow we managed to locate a little space between the test rigs to write reports etc. A common 2 HP fan accommodated in the adjoining toilet supplied the test rigs with air - we affectionately named the working spaces Trap 1, Trap 2, etc.

In this intimate environment we tested a number of Christopher's air-jet configurations. We determined the power requirements of an optimum air cushion using a simple jet. We managed to halve these by developing re-circulation systems adjacent to the jet. Eventually a large hut was erected in the garden of the White Cottage with a model workshop and we were able to build and test more ambitious rigs. As HDL expanded we eventually moved from the island to Hythe on Southampton Water in 1961 and carried out research into a number of hovercraft technology applications -not only for marine craft.

These included:-

a) The movement of large pieces of machinery and storage tanks

b) An over-land tracked hovercraft

c) The hover-bed which provided a comfortable support for patients recovering from severe burn injuries, on which it was proved that healing rate, was significantly improved.

Marine craft applications were split broadly into two types -the amphibious 'free of the surface craft' and sidewall hovercraft which were not amphibious but highly fuel efficient.

Regarding the amphibious hovercraft, Saunders-Roe had been given a contract from NRDC to build the experimental SRN1, which first hovered in the spring of 1959, and late that year crossed the English Channel on the 50th anniversary of Bleriot's famous flight on the 25th July. The event was big news and a euphoric press extrapolated the milestone success to craft that would soon cross the Atlantic and to speeds well beyond what was possible! However it was very encouraging and NRDC and Saunders-Roe agreed to gradually introduce passenger-carrying craft with basic research continuing at HDL and within the test facilities at Saunders-Roe.

Common to all these projects, the sea going craft and the so-called industrial applications, it became increasingly obvious that extra hover-height had to be attained without inordinate increases in lift power. So considerable effort was put into developing flexible skirts of minimal drag and maximum response to surface undulations. First semi-flexible skirts including the air-jets were tested but could only be fabricated using complex nut and bolt or rivet joints which were obvious wear points and were going to be very costly. Another much simpler alternative was an inflated loop at a slightly higher pressure than the cushion. This to a small degree was surface sensing and would initially move out of the way of small obstacles but impact with larger waves could produce areas of suction, which would force the craft to plough-in under certain conditions. It was also very vulnerable to damage.

The real breakthrough came with the invention of the finger-segmented skirt in 1962 by Denys Bliss, one of my co-senior engineers at HDL. This was indeed an Immaculate Conception. It was very simple to produce, was extremely responsive and would automatically tend to fill any gap caused by damage. The present state of the art includes a loop type seal for the upper flexible structure from which is suspended an array of finger segments for about three-quarters of the hover-height. Besides developing the configuration of flexible skirts, a large amount of research had to go into developing suitable materials. Avon rubber in Wiltshire pursued the problem to an acceptable solution. The continuous flexing and whiplash of skirt components riding over waves produces huge local accelerations which fatigues and peels the neoprene coating from the sandwiched reinforcement.

It was virtually impossible to simulate these conditions in the laboratory so most of the important testing had to be carried out on craft in service. Skirt maintenance was a major problem on busy ferry operations but gradually finger life increased from tens to hundreds of hours and upper flexible structures to several thousands. Recycling these components also increased these figures.

The amphibious hovercraft initially planted in the aircraft industry was constructed naturally with aircraft type materials and aircraft engines. With half the total installed power used to lift the craft off the surface, low weight was essential and aircraft engineering design and manufacturing processes seemed appropriate. The Rolls Royce Gnome and Proteus gas turbine engines were natural choices for the amphibious hovercraft and some considerable investment was made to marinise them for this purpose.

The amphibious capability demanded air propulsion. Special propellers had to be developed to absorb the power at much lower airspeeds than when used in aircraft. It was also necessary to try and reduce propeller tip speed, which was the main contributor to the craft's external noise.

The main financial support for development was allocated to the amphibious type of hovercraft with

NRDC and some from the Ministry of Defence funding further prototype craft such as the SRN2 and SRN3. Saunders-Roe was also undertaking design studies on a larger craft that they designated the SRN4. While this project was gradually being defined they decided to go into production on a smaller series of passenger craft, the SRN5 which was stretched to the SRN6. The first operation of these was on the Southsea to Ryde route with Hovertravel in 1963.

At the same time Vickers Armstrong at Swindon were also producing their own line of prototype amphibious craft - the VA1, VA2 and VA3. Like Saunders-Roe they also had paper studies of a larger craft to operate on the English Channel. But it became obvious to NRDC that the cost of developing a craft of this size could not be duplicated. Eventually British Hovercraft Corporation was formed to spur the development of this craft with shareholders of Westland (nee Saunders-Roe), Vickers and a small hovercraft manufacturer Cushioncraft with NRDC. Vickers soon fell by the wayside when the Westland designed SRN4 was the chosen channel craft.

As NRDC, through its subsidiary Hovercraft Development Ltd., was the licensing body for the use of the hovercraft patents, Christopher Cockerell and other senior management at HDL objected to what was in effect the founding of a monopoly organisation, which could if it so desired prevent other companies receiving licences to design, manufacture and sell. In the end it was resolved that NRDC left the board of BHC, but NRDC also removed Christopher as Technical Director of HDL. He continued to concentrate his efforts in lobbying government for financial support for the embryonic industry. Christopher's contribution was officially recognised when he was given his knighthood in 1969.

NRDC continued to support Westland and the world's largest hovercraft the SRN4 was completed, of which six were produced and operated on the English Channel routes for 32 years. It was developed through three mark numbers and as with most hovercraft series the initial design was stretched to a much larger craft than the prototype with an increase in payload of 80% which was achieved with only a 17% increase in power.

Around the time of the launch of the first SRN4, NRDC decided they could no longer maintain a technical group at HDL and its facilities and a large proportion of its staff were absorbed into the National Physical Laboratory. Although about a hundred SRN5 and SRN6's were sold, there were no further sales of the SRN4 craft. The main problems of high first cost (although somewhat commensurate with its extraordinary large work capacity), noise and the present investment of ferry operators in berthing facilities, worked against them.

Hovertravel, the pioneer operator on the Isle of Wight route, became aware that a new approach had to be initiated to take the amphibious hovercraft more into a marine design environment. This could be achieved with the smaller craft and Hovertravel with Westland and some support from NRDC introduced the AP1-88 in the 1980's. These were fabricated from welded marine light alloy and powered by air cooled diesel engines. Lower propeller tip speeds and thus lower noise levels were achieved by employing ducted propellers. This craft is now the only regular hovercraft in service in the UK with Hovertravel continuing their service from Southsea to Ryde on the I.O.W. Again, the 80-passenger prototype has been stretched to a capacity of 100. It is also used as a trainer craft for the military in the USA.

The United States have had their own hovercraft programmes mainly centred around military requirements, but it took them many years to finally agree to recognise the validity of Cockerell's patents. They poured enormous funds into prototype test craft and finally designed and manufactured 100 large amphibious landing craft capable of carrying a battle tank. You may have seen these being employed in the Gulf War and more recently in the Adriatic.

The most active company now producing hovercraft in the UK is Griffon Hovercraft in Southampton. They have at present full order books for craft to be used in a coastguard role.

I now have to turn the clock back to 1959 to recount the part played in the early development of the non-amphibious sidewall hovercraft, or as re-Christened in the USA -the Surface Effect Ship. Some of you may not be aware of this variant -essentially the general concept consists of a catamaran like configuration where the side-keels take no more than about 20% of the displacement, the aircushion supporting the remainder and with cushion seals confined to the bow and stern areas. This craft is therefore non-amphibious. Imagine my initial disappointment when Christopher Cockerell asked me to champion this version when I'd already been hooked on the hovercraft's amphibious capability. While still witnessing the remarkable amphibious trials of the SRN1 nearby, I was spending most of my time undertaking basic performance calculations of an aircushion-supported boat. And trying to perceive how this hybrid could compete with other high speed watercraft - planing craft, orthodox catamarans, hydrofoil craft and of course the amphibious hovercraft itself. It was of course this configuration, as I've already mentioned, that was a major stepping stone in Christopher Cockerell's inventive process.

Soon I proved at least that such a craft could out-perform high speed displacement craft. Based on this and the limited amount of testing that was being undertaken at the White Cottage, NRDC and HDL contacted William Denny and Brothers Ltd. of Dumbarton who at that time were famous for their ferry boat and river boat designs. What's more they were armed with a test tank. Denny's soon became licensees to the HDL patents and I found myself commuting quite frequently between the Isle of Wight and the Clyde.

It was essential to focus on a particular application and Denny's chose a riverboat operator in NE India who transported tea from the Assam valley down the Brahmaputra to Calcutta. Because of the currents and shallowness of the river places, a speed increase of only ten knots and a relatively shallow draft was a definite advantage and it was able to return up river in a fraction of the time. Working alongside Denny Naval Architects we optimised the proportions of a long barge like platform and undertook drag tests on the sidewall components. We decided that in order to investigate handling and other operational characteristics we would design and build a manned model of about 60 ft in length. Although the potential customer backed out of the project, the Denny's Board became more enthusiastic as the performance of the D1 indicated how little extra horsepower was required to increase speed significantly once hump conditions had been traversed. Hump is the speed at which maximum wave-drag is experienced.

The Board of Denny's decided to build a passenger river-craft the D2, which accommodated about 80 passengers at speeds of 20 to 25 knots. This vessel operated for some time on the Thames between Greenwich and Westminster after being delivered under its own power through the Scottish canals and down the East Coast in 1963! Three of these craft were built when sadly in 1963 Denny's went into voluntary liquidation based on a lack of orders for their 'bread and butter' ferry designs.

Appendix 2

Notes on the 'Denny Hovercraft' film
held by the Scottish Screen Archive

The original film was shot on Standard 8mm Kodachrome stock, as a purely unofficial and amateur record of events involving Denny Hovercraft Ltd. and the Leven shipyard at Dumbarton, and also including part of the voyage of Hovercraft D.2-002 to London, with a spell on board when the craft was operated by Thames Launches Ltd. The film was shown on several occasions to members of the Denny staff and many times over succeeding years before being gifted to the Scottish Screen Archive in May 2002, with copyright still being held by the Author for the time being. The film can be viewed free of charge on the Scottish Screen Archive web site, as follows: Type http://ssa.nls.uk into a search engine and click on 'Scottish Screen Archive' to get the Home Page; then type 6005 into the 'Quick Search' box at the top right-hand side and click 'Search'. This will bring up the film title **'DENNY HOVERCRAFT'**. Click on the title to access the 'Shotlist' and to view the film, regrettably now silent, displayed on the screen under the logo of The National Library of Scotland and the Scottish Screen Archive. (At the time this is being written the film clip is limited to events immediately prior to and during the voyage to the Crinan Canal and along the Caledonian Canal to Inverness).

Due to the small format of the original film the clarity of the images is not of the high definition standard that has become normal in 2013. Nevertheless, the film does form a memorable moving image record of the dramatic events surrounding Denny Hovercraft Ltd. in the summer of 1963. If any reader of this book wishes to watch the film on-line, the description of the voyage to Inverness can be taken from the Shotlist on the website and from Chapter 6, 'The Voyage of D.2-002 to London'.

It is possible to purchase a DVD of the complete film by contacting the Scottish Screen Archive, 39-41 Montrose Avenue, Hillington Park, Glasgow G52 4LA Tel. 0845 366 4600. Purchasing the DVD requires the applicant to complete a release form. Alternatively, by using the 'Getting Copies' information on the Archive website at http://ssa.nls.uk/index.cfm?sid=01.08 (This includes the option to buy directly online using PayPal or a credit card).

It is necessary to note here that the film was never completely finished, with an appropriate 'The End'. The reason for this is that, even having aligned the 8mm camera with great care when filming titles and similar material, the Author never knew if what was on the film was correct until the film had been returned from the processer. The attempt at filming 'The End' was very unsatisfactory and with the Author having joined Vickers Hovercraft Division it was never possible to have another attempt. The proper end of the film is after the sequence showing *Cutty Sark*, the Froude plaque on the wall of the Experiment Tank, and finally the name 'Denny' over the main entrance gate on the front of the Denny office building. This is followed by some scrap footage, most but not all of which should have been removed by the Author before the film was given to the Archive.

Thanks are due to Curator Ann Cameron of the Scottish Screen Archive for suggesting other films likely to be of interest to readers of this book, accessed by the procedure described above, using the Archive reference numbers:

HOVERCRAFT TEST (ref. 3201) This short film is of the Denny D.1 craft.

HOVERCRAFT (ref. 5199) Short film of D.2-002, with good detail of the controls on the craft bridge.

DENNY-BROWN STABILISER (ref. 4504)

DENNY CLOSURE (ref. 2157)

BIRTH OF A SHIP (ref. 0464)

A further recommendation is that the reader should view another film via the Scottish Screen Archive web site. This is the superb documentary **SEAWARD THE GREAT SHIPS**, which can be viewed free and in its entirety by following the procedure described for the 'Denny Hovercraft' film. 'SEAWARD THE GREAT SHIPS' (ref. 2230) dates from 1960, and gives an insight into many aspects of the huge industry that existed on the Clyde when William Denny Brothers were developing their Hovercraft.

ISBN 978-0-9926652-0-3

9 780992 665203